Story Time At The Altar

86 Messages For Children

Elaine M. Ward

CSS Publishing Company, Inc., Lima, Ohio

STORY TIME AT THE ALTAR

Copyright © 2002 by
CSS Publishing Company, Inc.
Lima, Ohio

Library of Congress Cataloging-in-Publication Data

Ward, Elaine M.
  Story time at the altar : 86 messages for children / Elaine M. Ward.
    p. cm.
  ISBN 0-7880-1955-4 (pbk. : alk. paper)
  1. Children's sermons. I. Title.
  BV4315 .W28 2003
  252'.53—dc21

                                                              2002151408

For more information about CSS Publishing Company resources, visit our website at www.csspub.com or e-mail us at custserv@csspub.com or call (800) 241-4056.

ISBN 0-7880-1955-4   PRINTED IN U.S.A.

For Ellie Morrison
who enfleshed for me the
"good news" of God,
because she was there

Table Of Contents

Holy Days And Sacraments

Jesus

Prayer

Introduction

We tell stories at the altar to enflesh the "good news of God" by being there and sharing stories of God's love and grace.

"He (Jesus) did not speak to them except in parables ... " (Mark 4:34).

"How are they to hear without someone to proclaim him?" (Romans 10:14).

"How beautiful ... are the feet of those who bring good news" (Isaiah 52:7).

"He shall feed his flock like a shepherd ..." (Isaiah 40:11).

This is a book of parables to tell to children *at the altar*, or home, school, camp, and so on. I have heard many who question "children's time," but as an educator-preacher-storyteller, my experience is that this is an enjoyable, educational moment within the community of faith.

Jesus told stories. The scripture is a sacred story of God, and children love stories. Having told stories to children for over forty years, this collection is for those who are committed to "feeding" the whole flock in the worship of God. As a storyteller, I believe in the power of the sacred story. As John wrote, "These stories were written so that you might know...."

The disciples came to Jesus, asking, "Who is greatest in the kingdom of heaven?" They didn't ask, "Who is the greatest — Socrates, the wise man? J. Paul Getty, Bill Gates, or Oprah, the rich? Meryl Streep or Mel Gibson, the entertainers?" They said, "Who is greatest in the kingdom of heaven?" and that makes all the difference, because the "kingdom of heaven" is the "action" of God. Jesus replied, "Unless you become like children, you will never enter the kingdom of God." He added, "Whoever humbles himself like this child, he is the greatest in the kingdom of heaven." Then he went ahead and showed us.

Have you ever had a child put his or her arms around you and say, "I love you"? Of such is the grace of God, the kingdom of heaven. When the child hugged her sad father, he said, "Stop, you're hugging me to death!" She replied, "No, Daddy, I'm hugging you to life!"

Weary from preaching or teaching, or leading worship Sunday after Sunday? Then look into the eyes of a child, share a smile, give a hug ... for of such is the kingdom of heaven.

Recently I went to the post office to purchase postage stamps. The clerk was excited by a new stamp. I was unimpressed but bought them because of her enthusiasm. For me a stamp is to send, as a hole is to dig, or a car is to drive. But a story ... a story is ...

To plant seeds of hope and possibility

When we love stories and books, we want to pass on their enchantment to the young. C. S. Lewis wrote, "Do you think I am trying to weave a spell? Perhaps I am; but remember your fairy tales. Spells are used for breaking enchantments as well as for inducing them. And you and I have need of the strongest spell that can be found to wake us from the evil enchantment of worldliness which has been laid upon us for nearly a hundred years."[1]

To share the beliefs and behavior of the people we belong to

"Once upon a time ..." and we see common objects — seeds, yeast, a woman who lost a coin — that represent the kingdom of God. We become the wounded stranger, the lost sheep, the person with one talent, the merchant who found a pearl, heard the voice of God at Jesus' baptism, the call to the disciples, the temptations of Satan, the stilling of the storm at sea, wandering through the wilderness, the doubt of Thomas, the fear of Peter, the healing of the invalid. Jesus, God's parabler, turned abstract, conceptual, systematic doctrine into concrete, living language. It is not surprising the Fourth Gospel begins, "In the beginning was the Word...."

To enjoy, enter, and experience vicariously

I was a guest preacher, preaching a narrative sermon at the early morning worship service, when the youth choir sang. I was surprised to see the youth file into the front pews for the second worship service, the traditional eleven o'clock service. At the close of worship I asked them why they had attended worship twice. They replied, "We like to hear stories!"

To become aware of and appreciate wonder, mystery, and a reverence for life and creation

Story wears many hats. Sometimes she sits beside the sick bed, holding our hand to speak her healing words. Sometimes she excites us with the telling of her travels. Quests, adventures, ordinary experiences suddenly become extraordinary. Other times she gathers her children around her, weaving them into a whole and introducing them to Wisdom, Wonder, and Reverence for life.

To connect head and heart with God, others, and creation

Stories are important ways of suggesting alternatives of belief and behavior, providing both the security of the familiar and the adventure of the new. As storytellers we are not only the makers of bridges to connect God's stories with the stories children hear and live, we are also the bridge itself, being there, with the children.

To ignite the imagination and invite song and laughter and community

When I was an only child in a house full of adults and was lonely, the story would take me by the hand and be my companion to new places, new things, new experiences. When I was hurting, the story held me, hugged me, healed me. Stories shaped who I was and helped me dream whom I would become. They reassured my longings and created new ones.

As an adolescent, being short on self-esteem, stories provided me with "happy endings." Sometimes they helped me wait. Sometimes they helped me celebrate, for stories have the power to ignite imagination to dream and hope and heal.

11

As a mother I entered stories with my sons to share enchantment together. When they left with their stories, I borrowed other children and told them stories, and on the way discovered adults too have a need for stories.

To become self-aware and discover our identity, meaning, and mission

"Hear, O Israel, the Lord, our Lord, is one God, and you shall love the Lord your God with all your heart and soul and mind and faith imagination. And you shall teach these stories to your children when you sit in the house and when you lie down and when you rise up, and when you do the dishes, make the beds, and ride in your second home, the automobile" (paraphrase Deuteronomy 6:4-9).

To provide resources, roots, and wings that form, feed, and transform faith, feeding the spirit

"The kingdom of God is like a story, which, when sown upon the soul, is the smallest of all the stories on earth, yet when it is warmed by wonder and watered with imagination, it grows up and becomes the meaning of Existence, and puts forth a World of Possibility so that the creatures of the earth can make their homes in it" (paraphrase Mark 4:30, 32).[2]

To see the sacredness of the ordinary and be with God

In the beginning was the Word and the Word became Story, enfleshing the plans and promises of God, a story of Love creating out of mud or star, Love on a leaky boat, Love in the wilderness or in the belly of a big fish, a burning bush, a wrestling, and a dusty manger, Love in a story calling us to love.

To experience the congregation's symbolic gesture that children belong to God, their family, and the family of the church

Children learn through stories that train the habits of the heart. The scripture reading was John 5:1-9. It was the text for the sermon that I preached that morning. I told the story again in the sermon. I even closed the worship service by retelling the same story. When I met with the children afterward, gathered for church school, I asked how many of them had been in worship and heard the sermon. Hands were raised. "How many of you heard a story?" Hands were lowered. So I told the story again for all of the children. We then lined the story so they could learn to tell it "by heart." Halfway through the story, I saw smiles begin to spread across the faces of those who had been at worship, as they remembered and cried out, "That's the story we heard in church!" Yes, that's the story we tell *at the altar.*

To comfort, challenge, and correct

The soul prefers story over reason, imagination over intellect, and encourages us to hope and cope, think and feel, dance and sing, speaking to our heart and our head to comfort, challenge, and correct.

To give "answers"

The people in the Bible looked for God and in their trust and confusion, their poems of lament and praise, they heard a voice. Listening for answers, the voice says, "I did not ask you to understand, I asked you to love." So we weave our worries, hopes, and pains into stories of trust in God.

To model faith, hope, and love

Jesus told stories of the last becoming first, the lost being found, the kingdom of God within and among us. His parables transformed doubt into joy, fear into faith, terror into trust. Through his stories we find hope and celebrate the blessing of life.

To suggest and show rather than lecture and scold

After eons of God speaking through the prophets, priests, and poets, God said, "I will show them," and Jesus, the Word, the incarnation of God, was born.

The story told at children's time, separated from the sermon by a hymn and scripture lessons, gives the story room to plant its seed and the preacher to expand and enter it more fully. At other times a story might introduce the sermon or conclude it.

One Easter worship the trumpets proclaimed Christ's resurrection. The music filled the sanctuary as one young child, feeling the joy of the place and the story, listening to the choir singing its praise to God, suddenly stood up on his pew to see. He began to move his arm, as if directing the choir, for in music and movement he had found his meaning of Easter as he sat among the sober, sedate adults. He celebrated the incredible news of new life! That is, until his parent pulled him down into his seat and scolded him.

We tell stories *at the altar* to involve children in the "good news" of God's incredible grace and unconditional love.

---

1. C. S. Lewis, *The Weight of Glory and Other Addresses* (New York: Macmillan, 1949).

2. Elaine M. Ward, *Love in a Lunchbox: Poems and Parables for Children's Worship* (Nashville, Tennessee: Abingdon Press, 1996), p. 7.

John The Baptist
Matthew 3:1-12

There was once a man named John. He lived in the wilderness, the desert. He wore the skins of a camel and had long hair that was never cut. He ate wild honey and locusts, which are a flying insect.

Some people eat fried ants and like them the way you and I like pizza. I can imagine John building a fire and frying locusts. But what was special about John was that he baptized and was called John the Baptist.

(Decide if you will digress here to talk about baptism or continue the story.)

What was really special was that John the Baptist baptized Jesus. He said to the people, "I baptize you with water but one who is more powerful than I is coming after me and he will baptize you with the Holy Spirit. I am preparing a way for him."

Talk together: For whom was John the Baptist preparing? (*Pause*) This is the season of "Advent" when we prepare for celebrating the birth of Jesus.

It's almost Christmas, I can't wait ...
In four weeks we celebrate
The angels' singing,
The wise men bringing
Their gifts of frankincense and myrrh and gold,
The shepherds' running,
The Christ Child coming,
As we hear his birthday story told.

Prayer: Dear God, we thank you for Christmas, the birth of Jesus Christ, and for John the Baptist who prepared his way. Amen.

15

Animals At The Manger
Luke 2:8-16

(Children like to make noise. They enjoy participating in storytelling by making noise, "sound effects." This Advent, invite your children to be the "animals" around the manger, as you tell the Nativity story.)

Joseph and Mary entered the barn out of the dark night. They could hardly see inside, but they could hear.

They heard a cow *moooo.*

(Invite the children to make "mooing" sounds.)

As they fed their donkey hay, after his long trip to Bethlehem, he said, *"Hee haw."*

(Make "hee-hawing" sounds.)

The moon shone through the window of the barn onto the rafter above the manger. They saw a dove and heard it *coooo.*

(Make "cooing" sounds.)

They felt something soft and wooley and wondered what it was until they heard ... *(Let the children guess.)* ... the lamb *baaaa.*

(Make "baaing" sounds.)

Praising God in the dark barn where Jesus was born.

(Ask the children for their suggestions of other animals that might be in the barn if Jesus were born today — chicken, duck, dog, cat, pig, and so on.)

Prayer: Thank you, God, for animal pets, for those who help people work and for those who give their lives for food. Help us care for them, especially those whose species are in danger. Amen.

The Christmas Star
Matthew 2:2

Once, long ago, a new star was born in the sky. Because it was a new star it was very small. Being small, the star was frightened of the large, dark night.

The other stars laughed and mocked it: "Afraid of the dark!" "Stars shine in the dark!" "Stars *love* the dark!"

The small star asked, "What is 'love'?"

"Love?" "Love?" "Love?" The stars could not explain.

One old star, however, so old its light was dimming, said, " 'Love' is shining bravely in the dark to give light. That is the purpose of stars."

"Will you teach me 'love'?" the small star asked.

"It is hard to teach love. There is no formula. You feel it; you do it. Come. I will *show* you love."

As the old star and the new star began their journey across the sky, the small star asked, "Where are we going?"

"I am leading you, as I led the shepherds ... to Bethlehem," and the old star told its story:

"Once, long ago angels came to say,
'Good news, dear friends, God's special Son is born
and will be found in a manger, in the hay.'
The angels sang and then the angels went away.
When they were gone the night was still
And darkness covered the silent hill.
'Where? Where will we go?' the shepherds cried.
In the darkness, though they tried,
     they could not find the way.
'Do not be afraid,' the angel had said.
But in the darkness, how would they find
     the Baby's bed?
Then God, who planned it all,
     sent out God's call,

17

And I came to be the light that led the shepherds
  through the night.
Following my light they came to Bethlehem
  to worship him."

The old light spoke softer now, shone dimmer still until it shone no more. Its work was done.

It had shown (shone) God's love, the greatest love of all, the special baby in the manger stall.

Today, above our sanctuaries and our stables, the small star shines, leading us, as the shepherds, to God's Love.

Talk together: Have you ever been afraid in the dark? What helps give you courage? What did the old star teach the young?

Prayer: Dear Lord, we thank you for the light of the stars in the night and the sun in the day and for Jesus, "the light of the world." Amen.

Silent Night, Holy Night
Luke 2:1-20

"Thank you, Pastor, for coming to visit my sick wife, especially on Christmas Eve," said the old man, as he shook hands with Franz Gruber, his minister, at the door.

When the pastor walked out into the night, he looked at the earth sprinkled with white snow and the sky with shining stars. It was a beautiful, silent, and holy night. If he hurried, there would still be time to write his Christmas Eve sermon. It had been such a busy day, and then this last minute call to come.

"Whoa," he cried, bringing his horse to a halt and taking a piece of paper from his pocket. The words flowed from his heart to the paper, as he wrote, "Silent night, holy night, all is calm, all is bright."

It seemed the night was filled with music. On such a night Jesus was born. In his imagination he saw young Mary and the baby Jesus and he wrote,

"Round yon virgin mother and child,
Holy infant so tender and mild,
Sleep in heavenly peace.
Sleep in heavenly peace."

Pastor Gruber blew on his hands. It was cold, but not until he had written would he replace his gloves on his hands and call for the horse to move on.

When Pastor Gruber got to church, he quickly ran to his office and wrote:

"Silent night, holy night,
Shepherds quake at the sight,
Glories stream from heaven afar,
Heavenly hosts sing Alleluia!
Christ the Savior is born!
Christ the Savior is born!"

The time passed swiftly. One by one the people came out of the darkness into the small, lighted church. Pastor Gruber sat at the organ. This Christmas his gift to the Christ Child and to his congregation would be his song of praise for that first silent, holy night.

Pulling out the organ stops, he placed his hands on the keyboard, but it had been so cold in the church, the notes were stuck. "Nothing will spoil this evening," Pastor Gruber thought, and he prayed, "God, help me," as he looked out at the congregation gathered to celebrate the holy birth.

Then suddenly he smiled, slid off the organ seat, and walked quickly to his office. When he returned, he sat on the altar step and began to strum his guitar.

"Silent night ... holy night ... wondrous star, lend thy light ...
With the angels let us sing Alleluias to our King,
Christ the Savior is born! Christ the Savior is born!"

For Pastor Gruber and his congregation, it was indeed a holy night!

Prayer: God, bless this night, night of all nights, for us all. Amen.

The Christmas Tree
John 1:5

Martin Luther stood silently under the cold, starry night, surrounded by the fir and pine trees of the forest, thinking of the night Jesus was born. The moon cast its shining light on the snow below. It was too beautiful, nature's echo of God's glory. Speechless, he held his breath and thought, "How can I share the beauty of this night, of this light?"

When Martin Luther returned home that night, his children cried, "Papa, Papa, what do you have?" as he set up the forest's pine tree beside the blazing fire in the fireplace. Then placing small candles on each branch of the tree, he lit them, bringing the light of the night within. "Oh, Papa," Anna exclaimed, "they are like the star that shone above the stable the night that Jesus was born!" The family stared at the Christmas tree and its light, and their hearts were filled with the light that "shines in the darkness," God's blessing of love at Christmas.

(*Uncover a small, lighted tree, at the end of the story.*)

Silent the night and holy, too,
He walked among the fir,
While shining silver stars dropped low
To set each snowy branch aglow,
Small gifts of heaven,
As gold and frankincense and myrrh.
He took the tree of evergreen
Into his home to share
The beauty of the starry nights
By substituting candle lights
On Jesus' birth,
The symbol of God's loving care.

Prayer: God, we thank you for lights that shine in darkness and for your loving care. Amen.

Christmas Eve
Luke 2:1-20

Call To Worship:
"Let us go now to Bethlehem and see this thing that has taken place, which the Lord has made known to us."

Leader:
With eager expectation
In great anticipation
We have waited for this night.
With glowing adulation
We join with God's creation
To see anew the wondrous sight,
The birthday of this newborn King,
While heaven and earth and angels sing.

While the congregation joins in singing a Christmas hymn, a child carrying a large star attached to a pole enters, coming down the central aisle, to place the star in a container. The choir and children follow into the semi-lighted church. Having been invited beforehand to bring their favorite stuffed animal, the children come to the altar area where they are to provide the animal sounds as the poem is read:

On Christmas Eve it has been said,
Inside the stable, 'round his bed,
Animals kneel to give God praise.
Then one by one they stand to raise
Their "alleluias" to their King.
In their own way the animals sing:
    The horses *neigh*,
    The doves *coo*,
    The sheep bleat, "*Baaaa*,"
    The owls cry, "*Whoooo*,"

The dogs bark, "*Woof*,"
The cats *meow*,
The mice make *squeaks*,
"*Mooo*," moans the cow,
The cricket *creaks*,
The chickens *cluck*,
The goose cries, "*Quack*,"
So does the duck.
On Christmas Eve, around his bed,
The animals speak, or so it's said.

Prayer:

The gift of love begins in the heart,
In the thought of the one who cares,
In the time that it takes to think and plan
For the love that the giver shares.
The gift of love is a simple gift,
No matter how large or small,
For the givers offering themselves
Is the greatest gift of all.

Dear God, we thank you for this gift of love you have placed in our hearts. May it grow to your glory. Amen.

The Donkey
1 Corinthians 4:10

"We are fools for the sake of Christ...."

Think of the donkey,
The one we call "dumb,"
Yet patient, mild and meek,
Carrying the very Child,
The Word that God would speak.

Twice-blessed he bore him on his back
Through the Jerusalem street
Amid the shouts of triumph,
Palm branches at his feet.

Silently he trod his way
And every step he took
Spoke aloud the donkey's praise.
And when the rest forsook
Their Lord that fateful day
On which he died,
Some thought they heard creation roar.
It was only a donkey that cried.

Lord, make me, as the donkey, meek
And hear me as I pray,
"May thy Kingdom come
On this holy Christmas Day."
Let me carry you in my heart
And with the donkey sing,
"Alleluia, Christ is born,
My Savior and my King!"

Prayer: Dear God, hear our prayer on this holy day, make and use us, as the donkey on whom Mary and then Jesus rode, humble and meek and mild. Amen.

Little Wind
Luke 2

Little Wind floated silently to the foot of God's throne. "Little Wind, I am sending my Word to Earth tonight in the form of a Baby and I need your help."

Little Wind let out a puff of excitement. It was warm air because it came from a heart on fire with love. Little Wind asked, "What can I do?"

"First, I want you to blow the angels closer to Earth. Then I want you to blow their songs through the heavens so the shepherds will hear the angel's words, 'Do not be afraid!' "

Little Wind blew and blew and the world was wrapped in the sound of singing.

"Now blow upon the stars so their light announces the coming of Light to all people."

Little Wind blew and blew and there was light, and the world glowed with the glory of God.

"Now blow this one star to where the wise men are to lead them to the Child to bring their gifts of love."

Little Wind blew and blew, wondering what gift he could bring. Following the shepherds into the stable, he felt the warmth of the animals' breathing and heard the baby cry. Mary wiped the brow of the baby, as Joseph fanned the child with a leaf.

Then Little Wind smiled and blew his breeze gently through the barn. The baby stopped crying. The mother smiled. The father rested, and all of them thanked God for sending Little Wind who gave the best gift of all — himself.

Prayer: Dear God, help us give ourselves to you and to others. Amen.

The Gifts
Matthew 2:11

"Where are the gifts?" the first wise man asked the other two wise men. All day they had traveled through the wind storm with sand in their eyes, their ears, and their mouths. Nestled close to the camel on which he had ridden all day, he called to the others, "Where are the gifts? Are they safe?"

"I have them," the second wise man called back, as he brought the gold, the crown, and the book of the Law to the campfire, placing them on the ground.

"There would be no need for this long journey, if we should lose the gifts for the Child," replied the third wise man.

"Oh, simply to see him, to be with him would be enough!" the other two exclaimed.

The men were tired, the camels too welcomed the rest, and they all slept until the first wise man awakened them. "It is time to go on. The star is leading us."

When at last they came to the place of the Child, they fell down and, giving him their gifts, they worshiped him.

Now when Jesus, the Child, was grown, he came to John to be baptized and the Spirit led him into the wilderness where he was tempted by the devil for forty days and nights.

The devil said, "If you are the Son of God, change this stone into a loaf of bread. Show your power."

Jesus took the gift of gold he had been given by the three kings and threw it to the ground, saying, "We do not live by bread or gold, but by the living word of God."

The devil then led him up the mountain and said, "See all the kingdoms of the world. I can make you king. Worship me!"

Jesus took the gift of the crown he had been given by the three kings and tossed it down the mountain, saying, "I will worship and serve only God!"

Then the devil took Jesus to Jerusalem, to the top of the temple and said, "If you are the Son of God, throw yourself to the ground, for it is written God will protect you."

Jesus took the book of the Law and flung it far from the temple, saying, "Do not put God to the test. Trust God alone!"

Then Jesus, filled with the power, love, and word of God, returned to Galilee, saying, "Lord, thy will be done."

Talk together: What were the gifts the wise men brought the baby in the story from the Bible? What were the gifts in the story we just read? Why did the author change the gifts?

Prayer: Dear Lord, let us hear your word through all the stories, so we may live in the presence of your love and will. In the name of Jesus, whom we call Christ. Amen.

Creation
Genesis 1:1—2:3

In the beginning God created Earth. One day Earth thought, "Wouldn't it be wonderful if there were humans to enjoy and celebrate my beauty?"

However, Earth, created by God, could not create humans, so Earth told God her idea and God thought that it was a good one. God took some of the clay out of Earth and breathed it alive, and having created from Earth, from *humus*, called them "humans."

Then God decided that God would be their home when they died, but because Earth thought up the idea of humans in the first place, she would be their home while they lived. But God could not let go of what God had created in love and became the home of humans here on Earth, as well.

There are many creation stories. Another says: In the fullness of time there was a great, silent, magnificent, burning ball of fire, the universe filled with energy. And God shouted, "Let there be!" and the burning fireball exploded and sparks flew out into the empty space and there was light. And it was good. From that ball of fire came stars and galaxies, mountains and seas, flowers and trees, and millions of years later, people, aware of the beauty and wonder of the universe. And it was good. From the people came sacred stories of God's love and their worship of God. And in the fullness of human time a man called Jesus of Nazareth was born, sent from God to show us God's love. And it was very good.

Talk together: Can you tell us another story of creation? Read from Genesis.

Prayer: God, we thank you for the earth and all its creatures and pray that you will help us learn how to care for it and do it. Amen.

Moses, The Baby
Exodus 1:8—2:10

Once upon a time there was an evil king who ordered that all boy Hebrew babies were to be killed. So when the baby Moses was born, the mother made a waterproof basket, put the baby in it, and said to his sister, Miriam, "Keep the baby safe!"

Miriam did as her mother said and hid Moses in the river. One day the king's daughter came to the river to bathe and found the baby. He was crying, so she picked him up and comforted him, thinking, "This must be a Hebrew baby."

When Miriam saw this, she was afraid, for her work was to keep the baby safe. Miriam took a deep breath, said a quick prayer, "God, help me!" and waded into the water toward the princess. "Shall I get the baby a nurse from the Hebrew women?" she asked.

The princess said, "Yes, my child." Miriam called her mother, and when Moses was old enough, they brought him to the princess who gave him his name because, as she said, "I drew him out of the water."

Talk together: What do you know about Moses? How did Miriam take care of her baby brother?

Prayer: Dear God, we thank you for familes who love and care for each other. Help us remember that we are all one family and part of your creation. Amen.

Moses, The Man
Exodus 3:1-4

"It's burning!" Moses exclaimed, looking at the bush burning before him. "Who started the fire?" Moses was talking to himself because there was no one else there. But suddenly Moses heard, "Moses!" Moses shook his head. Being alone in the wilderness so long must have affected his hearing, for bushes do not speak.

Nor do bushes burn unless someone starts a fire. Moses was confused. Moses was worried. Moses was afraid.

"Moses, take off your shoes," the voice said. "You are standing on holy ground." Moses wondered how this land was holy because here they worshiped Pharaoh the king instead of God.

The voice said, "I have heard my people's prayers. I am sending you to the king to let my people go."

Now Moses was really afraid. The king was powerful. He could kill Moses. Moses protested, "But the king will not listen to me. He will kill me."

The voice said, "I will be with you. I, the Lord, your God!"

Now Moses was really, really afraid and hid his face. He was afraid to look at God and he took off his shoes, for he knew he was in the presence of God.

Talk together: Why was Moses afraid? What makes you afraid? All of us have fears, and God said to Moses, "I will be with you."

Prayer: Dear God, thank you for being with us to give us courage and guidance, comfort, and love. Help us hear your voice and remember that wherever you are is holy ground. Amen.

David And Goliath
Psalm 63

The lion slowly approached the sheep, who, eating the grass, was unaware of the lion about to eat him. David, the shepherd boy, taking care of the sheep, leaped to his feet, grabbing his slingshot as he did. Placing five small, smooth, sharp stones in his slingshot, he slung them through the air at the lion. As David held his rescued sheep, his heart pounded. Now he had time to be afraid. So sitting beside the flowing stream, he picked up his harp to calm his heart, singing his praise to God: "The Lord is my shepherd. I shall not want." As David sang, it seemed the hills echoed his praise to God whose "steadfast love is better than life."

"Fee! Fie! Foe! Fum! I smell the blood of a Hebrew son!" the giant, Goliath, roared and the earth shook, as David, the small boy, stood before the giant! He wore no armor. It was too heavy for a small boy. He had no sword, only a slingshot and five smooth stones, wet from the brook, but he had trust in God.

David had killed a lion. Now David killed a giant. David, the young shepherd boy, became the courageous champion of his people, for Goliath, like the lion, wanted to devour his people.

Talk together: What do you like best about this story? David didn't pick the fight with Goliath, but he didn't run from him either. How did he prepare himself? All of us have "giants" to fight. What "giant" did Martin Luther King, Jr., fight? Gandhi? Jonas Salk? They fought their giants as Jesus fought his, because they knew God. David was small, but he was brave and outwitted his giant because God was with him.

Prayer: Lord, give us courage and guidance to conquer our "giants," because we know you are with us. Amen.

Elijah And The Voice
1 Kings 19:11

Elijah was a messenger of God. One day the word of the Lord told him, "Go out and stand on the mountain before the Lord." Now there was a great wind, so strong that it was splitting mountains and breaking rocks in pieces before the Lord.

(Pass a large sea shell or empty jar, inviting the children to take turns listening to the noise. Ask the others, while they are waiting, to put the palms of their hands on their ears and push, hearing the sound inside themselves. As they listen, continue telling the story.)

And after the wind came an earthquake. The ground shook and broke open, but the Lord was not in the wind nor the earthquake. And after the earthquake came a fire, but after the fire, a sound of sheer silence.

(Pour water into the jar so the children can hear the "sheer silence.")

Talk together: What did Elijah hear? Sometimes the voice of the Lord, the Spirit of God, speaks in silence. Have you ever heard a "silent" voice? Have you ever prayed with a silent voice? Pretend you are at the seashore and the bright sun is coming up over the water, or it's the end of the day and you watch the sunset, the sky painted pink. Have you ever said, "Thank you, God," silently?

Prayer: Let us pray now in sheer silence. *(Pray silently.)* Amen.

Job
The Book Of Job

Once upon a time there was a man named Job. One day his servant came running to Job and said, "Your donkeys, camels, goats, and sheep have been stolen and your servants killed." Job ran to his cattle, or where they had been, and it was true. He was sad to see his cattle gone and his servants killed. Then one of his friends ran to Job and said, "The wind blew your house down!" Job ran home, or where it had been, and it was true. He was sad to see his house gone. But when he saw that his house had fallen on his family, he cried. He pulled on his hair and tore his clothes, and sat on the ground for seven days and seven nights. His sadness was very great.

Then Job complained to God, for Job was a good man. He prayed and pleaded. He wanted an answer. Where was God when these awful things happened? His friends gave him answers, but they did not help. Job felt hopeless and sad. Why didn't God answer him?

Over and over Job called out to God. Over and over God was silent, and Job was very sad. Then one day a great whirlwind appeared and out of the whirlwind God said to Job, "Where were you, Job, when I created the heavens and the earth?" And at last Job was silent.

When God finished speaking, Job kneeled and confessed, "I did not understand things too wonderful for me. I had heard of you by the hearing of the ear, but now my eye sees you." Job praised his Maker.

Talk together: Have you ever wondered, "Where is God when bad things happen?" What do you think?

Prayer: Dear God, thank you for the song of the birds, the sounds of insects, the grass and the flowers, the stars and the moon, and all creation, showing us your wisdom, love, and imagination, especially Jesus, the Christ. Amen.

Samuel
1 Samuel 3

Once there was a boy called Samuel. Though Samuel was only a boy, he helped Eli in the temple. One night, when Samuel was sound asleep, he heard his name called. "Samuel! Samuel!" Samuel answered, "Here I am!" Then he ran to Eli. "Eli, Eli, did you call?" Eli said, "I did not call. Go to sleep, Samuel. It is late." Samuel did as Eli said and the voice called again: "Samuel! Samuel!" Samuel got up again and went to Eli. "Here I am!" he said, thinking that Eli had called him in his sleep. Eli was an old man and needed his sleep, so he answered, "I did not call. Lie down, Samuel, and go to sleep." But it was in his sleep that Samuel heard the voice. The third time he got up and went to Eli. "Here I am, for you called me." Now Eli was wide awake. "It is the Lord!" he said. "Samuel, go lie down and if you hear your name called again, say, 'Speak, Lord, for your servant is listening.'" So Samuel went and lay down in his place and when he heard his name called again, he did as Eli said. As Samuel grew, the Lord was with him and Samuel let none of his words fall to the ground, for Samuel was a trustworthy prophet of the Lord.

Talk together: There was once a man who would awaken in the middle of the night and he did not know why. He went to a counselor, a wise man he trusted, and told him about it. The counselor replied, "Perhaps God is calling you." The next night when he awoke in the middle of the night, he said, "Here I am!" and began to pray and write in his journal, remembering the story of Samuel.

Prayer: God, help us hear your call and remember your stories, especially the story of the boy Samuel. Amen.

"Do Unto Others"
Matthew 7:12

Once a week we go to the grocery store the day I get my allowance. Some of it I put aside for church and some I save and some I spend. When we go to the grocery store, Mom says I can choose. Of course Mom gets the final choice when we reach the check-out counter, but for now the choosing is mine.

My allowance began when Mom had to drive me back to the grocery store so I could tell the clerk I had "borrowed" a package of gum. It embarrassed Mom so much that at the next family council we all decided I was old enough for an allowance to learn the importance of the wise use of money.

Today I casually strolled past mounds of Mounds, Musketeers, and M and M's, motorcycle magazines, toy squirt guns, and 27 different brands of chewing gum.

It was then I saw her staring at the silver-wrapped chocolate kisses, simply staring. I stared too because I was trying to choose between those small chocolates wrapped in silver that I love or the gum backed by baseball cards that I collect.

I closed my eyes to imagine chewing the sticky, sweet gum or the rich, dark chocolate, and when I opened my eyes, I saw her slip the brown-wrapped candy bar into her coat pocket.

I wish I hadn't seen it. It's none of my business. Her mom can hold a "family council" and bring her back to the clerk with an apology! Right now I need to decide what I want, although actually I have plenty of time because Mom's shopping list is always long.

I hate "squealers." I wish I hadn't seen or she hadn't taken it! But why do I keep bumping into her? Seeing her is like my conscience, that "little voice inside," as my mom calls it, talking to me.

"NO, YOU CAN'T HAVE IT!" was heard throughout the store. It wasn't like my mom's quiet explaining, but a loud, angry, violent voice shouting. And there she was again, softly sobbing, shaking before her mother's shout and slap.

I guess that takes me "off the hook." Now I don't have to tell, but why do I feel worse than before? This "do unto others" sure is complicated.

"So what did you choose?" Mom asked, meeting me at the check-out counter.

"Nothing," I mumbled, moving the money in my pocket.

Talk together: What would you have done? Have you ever had such an experience of seeing someone tempted or of being tempted yourself? What did you do?

Prayer: Lord, "Lead us not into temptation." Or, what I really mean is, be with me to help me when I am tempted, and help me choose to do unto others what I would have them do to me. Amen.

Endless Peace
Isaiah 9:7

"His authority shall grow continually, and there shall be endless peace ... He will establish and uphold it with justice."

The children were playing happily in the room. The dogs barked. The cats meowed. The lions roared. Soon, however, the happy, noisy sounds became angry noises. "I'm the lion!" "No, I'm the lion!" "I am the lion! I was the lion first!" growled the child to show his power, as he was about to bite the other. But there was silence. The teacher waited for the growls to begin again. The other boys and girls stopped to see what would happen. What they heard was, "Why not two lions?" asked one of the fighters. "Two lions?" asked the other. "Two lions," they both agreed.

Talk together: Jesus, called the Prince of Peace, said, "Blessed are the peacemakers, for they shall be called the children of God." What are "peacemakers"? Have you ever met one? Have you ever been one? Tell us about it.

Prayer:
Help us, Lord, to plant a garden of peace together.
Flowers, not fear,
Marigolds, rather than missiles.
So that together we will choose life
So all may live. Amen.

Balance
Luke 5:15-16

A boy was walking down the road, tired, hungry, lonely, limping on his left foot. His hands in his pockets, he met an old grandmother who, seeing the sad look on the boy's face, cried out, "Heaven and earth were made for you, child!" Without thinking the boy lifted his shoulders and hopping on his right foot, began to whistle, until he came to a small bird, lying on the road with a lame limb. "What right have you to spoil my day!" the boy shouted at the bird. "Heaven and earth are made for me!" and he kicked the bird to the side of the road. He did not see the man walking toward him, but the man saw the boy kick the bird and said, "Dust you are and to dust you will return." The boy stopped and stared at the man, his shoulders falling, remembering his hunger, as he limped away on his left foot.

The boy walked for a long time. Then he sat down and took two pieces of paper out of his pocket and wrote on one of them: "Heaven and earth are made for me!" and on the other he wrote: "Dust you are and to dust you will return." When the boy finished writing, he stood up, put one paper in his left pocket and the other paper in his right pocket, and walked down the road with his right and his left foot in *balance*.

Talk together: Prayer supports and permits us to trust God, for life is like a teeter-totter. "Up" experiences are fun; the wind blowing through our hair, seeing new sights from the height. Then suddenly "down" again. What do you like best about prayer?

Prayer: God, sometimes we feel you are close and sometimes far away ... up and down. Help us remember your promise, "I will be with you." Amen.

A Little Child Shall Lead Them
Isaiah 11:6

During the winter months the church offered shelter for the homeless: dinner in the evening, sleep at night, and breakfast every morning. But by the third year it became harder and harder to find hosts.

The coordinator stood before the congregation asking for volunteers for three weeks in a row until at last a seven-year-old raised her hand and shouted, "I'll do it!"

Amanda's sign-up list to help filled up quickly, and when that night came, Amanda got there early, folded the napkins, set the tables, and greeted the guests at the door, welcoming them, the strangers, as a hostess to her home, telling them how glad she was that they had come, and asking their names.

When it was time to eat, Amanda invited all to stand and hold hands. Then she asked one of them to bless the food. One "stranger" volunteered.

Then Amanda requested, "Who would like to help serve the food?" and suddenly volunteers and guests became family, helping one another, for a little child had led them.

Talk together: What did Amanda do? Why do you think she did it? What would you like to do?

Prayer: Lord, help us remember those who have no homes and are hungry. Let us like Amanda "feed" them in whatever way we choose. Amen.

When He's Here
Psalm 23

It was Father's Day and the minister had gathered the children around him at the altar, including his own three-year-old son. These were his friends. Every Sunday they gathered to hear stories from the Bible, seated close to their pastor. Now he looked into their eyes and smiled, for he loved these children. Because it was Father's Day, he asked, "What do you like best about your daddy?" The children named one thing they liked about their father. When all of the children had spoken but his own son, he looked at Michael and asked again, to which Michael replied, "When he's here!"

Talk together: What do you like best about your father?

When my granddaughter Lauren was five, I stayed overnight at her house. Being an early riser, I quietly descended the stairs and found a place to read and drink my coffee. Then a sleepy-eyed five-year-old bumped down the stairs with her blanket, took the coffee cup from my hand and plopped into my lap, nestling, a bundle of blessing. "You woke me up," she said. But I had tiptoed down the stairs, puttered silently in the kitchen, so I refused the charge. She cuddled closer. "You woke me up," she said again. This time with wisdom I did not protest but asked her, "How?" "By being here. When you are here I want to be with you."

Who do you want to be with?

Prayer: Lord, we thank you for being with us, for giving us parents and people who love us. Help us show our love for them by wanting to be with them. Amen.

41

Treasures
Matthew 6:19-21

A stone worn smooth
In a sweaty hand,
A scrap of string,
A rubberband,
A chirping cricket,
Grains of sand ...
God, thank you for all the "treasures"
That you planned.

One day a seven-year-old girl packed her father's lunch. Along with his sandwich and apple and coffee she put her favorite stone, a small toy doll, and a marble, her "treasures." Her father, thinking it was junk, threw it away after he ate his lunch. When he came home that evening, she asked, "Where are my treasures?" "What treasures?" he asked. "Oh, I forgot to put in a note to tell you I was sharing my treasures with you because I love you, Daddy," she said, hugging her father. He returned to his office quickly and retrieved his daughter's "treasures," for she was saying in her way, "Here is the best I've got and I am sharing it with you."

Talk together: What is your favorite "treasure"? With whom do you share it?

Prayer: Dear God, we thank you for our "treasures," especially the greatest, which is your love. Amen.

The Secrets Of God
Psalm 148:5-12

When a child is in the mother's womb, God whispers to that child the secrets of the universe. Then the child in the womb hears God's stories: calling into existence the sun and moon and stars, separating the land from the waters, and creating rainbows and relationships. For nine months God reveals what there is to know of creation; then the child is ready to be born. In the excitement and joy of being born, of entering the world, the child forgets all the secrets, even the secret of God's love and presence, and the rest of the child's life is spent searching for those secrets once again.

Talk together: Do you know God's secrets? Can you tell us one of them? Do you think we ought to share God's secrets? I will whisper to you the greatest secret. (*Whisper "God loves you" in each child's ear and invite them to go out into the congregation to share with the grown-ups that "secret."*)

Prayer: Thank you, God, for stories that give us hope and for the "secret" of your love. Amen.

Breaking Branches
Romans 8:22

"We know that the whole creation has been groaning...."

There once was a poor woodcutter whose heart was full of love, but his stomach was very empty. In the winter he was cold, as well. But because he loved every living thing, he refused to tear off living branches in order to warm himself, for the sap, which is the blood of the tree, would drip, as if the tree were bleeding. One day the woodcutter was walking through the woods when he heard, "Sticky, sticky is my sap when my tender twigs are snapped."

The woodcutter stopped to listen. He looked up at the tree and saw the broken branch and the sap running down its bark. He tore off a piece of his shirt to use as a bandage to bind up the wound, and the tree poured down a shower of coins.

The woodcutter thanked the tree and returned to his home. That evening as he sat at his table, his greedy neighbor looked into his window and saw the pile of coins. He called through the window, "Where did you get all that money?"

The good woodcutter told him what had happened, and the greedy man did not even stop to say, "Thank you," as he ran to the pine tree in the woods. He heard, "Sticky, sticky is my blood. Touch me and you will receive a flood."

The greedy woodcutter had no time to listen to the warning but quickly grabbed a branch and broke it off, and the pine tree showered him with sticky sap. It was so sticky that the greedy woodcutter could not move. There he stayed for three days until the sap became soft enough for him to drag himself home where he sat in shame for three more days, thinking of his greed.

Talk together: How did the good woodcutter treat the tree? How did the greedy one treat the tree? In Paul's letter to the Romans, he wrote that the whole creation has been groaning. Do you think the earth is groaning now? Why? We have the choice to be a good woodcutter or a greedy one.

Prayer: Thank you, God, for your good creation. Give us the wisdom and boldness to care for rather than to harm the earth. Amen.

Trust In The Lord
Psalm 56:4

"O Most High, when I am afraid, I put my trust in you."

Peter was four and Peter had an older brother, Alan, who was ten. Peter followed Alan everywhere. He wanted to do whatever Alan did. He wanted to be just like Alan, and Alan was a swimmer.

Peter announced, "I want to swim!"

So Mother signed up Peter to take swimming lessons. David was his teacher.

"Peter, the first thing to learn is to trust the water and trust me," said David.

Peter could trust David. He was strong and he knew how to swim, but he wasn't sure he wanted to trust the water.

David said, "Lie back on the water as if it were your bed and I will hold you."

Over and over David held Peter on the water as if it were his bed. One day he said, "I am going to take away my hands and the water will hold you."

Peter trusted David's words, and the water held him while he "floated."

Talk together: Have you ever "floated" on water? Might prayer be like floating on water, trusting God?

Prayer: Lord, as birds float on the air, trusting, so I would trust your love and care. Amen.

The Eensy-Weensy Spider
Psalm 147:8b

Together the nursery children and I wondered at the beauty and importance of water as part of God's good plan. We washed the dishes and dolls, waded in paper puddles, made butter sandwiches for a seashore picnic, fished in a rocking boat while sharing a story of Jesus and his friends going fishing, and sang our thanks "for rain that comes falling" and "The Eensy-Weensy Spider."

"The eensy-weensy spider went up the waterspout,
Down came the rain and washed the spider out,
Out came the sun and dried up all the rain
And the eensy-weensy spider went up the spout again."

We sang with joy as I wondered, "Is this song *religious?*"
I listened to the words again and heard that the spider "went up." "Up" is forward, growing, moving.
But the rain came down and washed the spider out. Rain both provides growth as well as disappointment. Too much rain "floods" and destroys. So we learn to "swim" in the waters of life. Then "out came the sun" and we feel its warmth, remembering its dependability. The words plant "seeds" of hope, encouraging us to go "up the waterspout again" ... and again ... and again.

Talk together: What do you like best about rain? About sunshine? How is water part of God's plan? Which do you prefer, rain or sunshine? Why? Sing the song now with me.

Prayer: God, we thank you for the rain and for the sun, without which we could not grow. Amen.

47

Opened Eyes
Psalm 25:2

"O my God, in you I trust...."

Once upon a time a grandfather gave his granddaughter, about your age, not a pony, nor a puppy, nor a pretty dress, but a cup with dirt in it. He filled Dinah's toy teapot with water and said, "Every day pour a bit of water in the dirt in the cup."

So Dinah did. It didn't make any sense, pouring water into the dirt every day but Dinah loved her grandfather, so she did what he said. But soon she forgot. Sometimes she would have to get up out of her warm covers at night and in her bare feet cross the cold floor to water the dirt with her toy teapot.

Dinah asked her grandfather, "Is it time to stop?" He replied, "No." By the fourth week Dinah tried to give the cup back to her grandfather but he said, "Be faithful."

The next morning, when Dinah woke up, something was different. There was something green in her cup. Was it magic? Dinah went closer and saw two tiny green leaves coming up out of the dirt.

Day by day they grew. She could hardly wait to tell Grandpa. When Grandpa came, she cried, "Look! Look what grew!" But Grandpa knew. He said, "Life is hidden in the most surprising places."

"And, Grandpa, all it needed was water." Grandpa took Dinah on his lap. "No, Dinah, all it needed was trust and patience."

Talk together: Show a cup of dirt and ask, "What do you think is in here? What might happen? Why?" Is it hard to wait? To trust?

Prayer: Dear God, open our eyes so we may see more than what we see, that we may see your invisible spirit, your breath of life in all living things, and we give you thanks. Amen.

Timothy's Questions
Psalm 100:3a

"Who made it? How does it work? What is it for? Why is it here? Where did it come from? How did you get it?" Timothy liked to ask questions. It was the way he learned.

"Where are you going?" Timothy asked his mother.

Mother replied, "I am going to a meeting at church."

"Why?"

Mother explained what she would be doing.

"Bring me the hammer, Timothy," his father called, as the door shut and Mother left.

Timothy brought the hammer to his father, asking, "What are you doing?"

His father replied, "I am replacing the screen that Wags tore out."

"Why do you need the hammer?"

Father replied, "The hammer is used to pound the nails that hold the screen to the door."

"Who made the hammer?"

Father explained all that he knew about hammers.

The next day in school, as Timothy was washing his hands, he asked, "Where does the water go?"

His teacher said, "Let's find out."

Timothy and his teacher and the other boys and girls watched the water pour out into the sink. They looked at pictures of waterpipes in a book. They worked with pipes and tools. They visited the custodian and saw the waterpipes at school.

Throughout the day Timothy asked. Finding the bird's nest on the playground, he asked, "How do birds build nests?"

His teacher replied, "Let's find out."

They took the nest apart to see how and of what the nest was made.

When Timothy asked, "What makes a flower grow?" they planted a flower seed in a pot, put it in the sun, watered it each day, and watched the seed grow.

All because ... Timothy asked questions because Timothy wanted to know.

Talk together: Who answers your questions? We have a desire and need to know, to learn, to touch, taste, see, hear, and smell whatever is present. We are always learning about ourselves, about the world, and about the people in our world. What would you like to know?

Prayer: Dear God, thank you for creating us with curiosity and for people who answer our questions. Amen.

36 People
Matthew 22:36-39

Talk together: 36 is a special number for the Jewish people. Do you know why?

There is a story that says as long as there are 36 good people in the world, God will allow the world to go on.

Why 36? I don't know. But if there are fewer, they say the world will end.

Do you want to know who "they" are? No one knows but God. You might be one of them.

How can you tell? Even the 36 do not know. The 36 are the ones who care about those who hurt or are hungry or lonely. They have compassion, love, for all creatures.

Talk together: Might you be one of the 36?

If someone asked you to name one person for the list of 36, whom would you name?

Prayer: Dear Lord, thank you for your love and for the gift of life. Help us share our love and blessings with others. Amen.

The Eagle
Isaiah 40:31

A man found an eagle's egg and put it in the nest of a barnyard hen. The eaglet hatched with the brood of chicks and grew up with them. All his life the eagle did what the barnyard chicks did, thinking he was a barnyard chicken. He scratched the earth for worms and insects. He clucked and cackled. And he would thrash his wings and fly a few feet into the air. Years passed and the eagle grew very old. One day he saw a magnificent bird above him in the cloudless sky. It glided in graceful majesty among the powerful wind currents, with scarcely a beat of its strong golden wings. The old eagle looked up in awe. "What's that?" he asked. "That's the eagle, the king of the birds," said his neighbor. "He belongs to the sky. We belong to the earth — we're chickens." So the eagle lived and died a chicken, for that's what he thought he was.[1]

Talk together: Why didn't the eagle, king of the birds, fly? Some stories and books help us "fly," reminding us that we, as God's children, are divine, although we live among the "chickens of the earth."

Prayer: Lord, we thank you that we are, in a sense, "eagles," for we can "fly," in the sense of having hope in you and in your promises that we are your children. Amen.

---

1. Anthony de Mello, *Awareness* (New York: Doubleday, 1992), p. 3.

The Magic Thread
Psalm 118:24

"This is the day which the Lord has made."

When it was summer, the boy wanted winter, and in the winter, he dreamed of summer. In school he could hardly wait until he got home, and on Sundays, he longed for school to begin. He especially wanted to be older, but to be older requires time. So it was that in the woods where he would go walking, he met an old woman who knew of his dream and gave him a ball of a magic thread. All he needed to do was to pull the string and time would pass quickly. Soon he was pulling the string whenever he was unhappy or there was suffering or misfortune. With time the string turned from gold to silver to gray, as his hair turned from brown to gray to white. An old man now, walking in the woods, he met the woman who had given him the ball. Seeing how unhappy he still was, she gave him one wish, and he wished to live his life again without the ball. When he awoke he saw what a beautiful morning it was and enjoyed it all day.

Talk together: Have you ever wished as the boy did? Sometimes we are impatient. "If I could only read, then I would be happy." "If I were older, I could stay up later." "When I am bigger, they will let me play with them." We go on wishing and wishing when today is the day to enjoy.

Prayer: Dear God, help us be content with "what is." We thank you for the beauty of this day. Amen.

Can I Help You?
1 John 4:7

The young girl, her arms full of books, crossed the park, seeing the old man sitting on a bench. She thought to herself, "It must be strange to be old and sit in the cold on a small park bench in a great overcoat." Just then the old man lifted his head and saw the girl watching him. He asked, "Yes?" The girl stammered, "I just thought ... I wondered ... do you need ... can I help you?" The old man smiled and said, "You already have."

A man was sitting in the hospital waiting room, tears rolling down his cheeks, his shoulders rising and falling as he sobbed, then moaning. The people in the waiting room were uncomfortable, not knowing how to respond, when a small child squirmed loose from her mother's arms. The toddler played with the ashtrays, the water fountain, the magazines, and finally stopped in front of the sobbing adult. She watched as the tears continued to roll down his face, and then she reached her hand out to touch his face, wipe the tears from his cheeks, and say gently, "All right, all right, all right." The man opened his eyes and saw the child. The shape of his mouth changed slowly. He gently caught her hand between his wrinkled fingers and kissed it.

Talk together: How did the girl in the park help the old man? How did the toddler? Why did they do it?

Prayer: Dear Lord, Jesus taught us to love and showed us how. Thank you for your love through Jesus, our Friend and Redeemer. Amen.

"Good News"
Matthew 11:2-11

John the Baptist, preparing the way for Jesus, found himself in prison for telling the truth, and he sent word to his disciples to find out if Jesus really was the one for whom they had waited.

They came to Jesus and he answered them, "Go tell John that the blind can see, the lame walk, the deaf hear, and the poor have good news preached to them."

A child once went to Sunday school with a nickel and a quarter in his pocket. The quarter was for the offering.

The leader announced, "Boys and girls, your money this morning is going to Blair House, the home for children who are not as blessed as you with mental abilities."

The leader continued, but Alan stopped listening, because Alan did not want to be there. Because of Sunday school and Mom, he had had to miss the lake trip with his best friend. "It's not fair! I have to go to school all week and then on Sunday too."

Alan was still feeling sorry for himself and complaining when Susan handed him the offering basket. Alan reluctanly put his hand in his pocket and felt the nickel and the quarter. "Humph!" he said, placing the nickel in the basket. "I deserve the quarter for having to come!"

The incident was quickly forgotten as the class began to prepare to act out the story of John the Baptist in prison.

The following Sunday the leader said, "I have called your parents and they have given me permission to take you all to visit Blair House this morning."

"Hey, great, no sitting and listening!" Alan thought.

When they arrived everyone felt like strangers. Then suddenly one of the children from Blair House began to sing, "Jesus loves me, this I know," and everyone joined him. Soon they were all singing and playing games together. "These kids are neat," Alan whispered to Susan.

Before they knew it, it was time for the class to return to church. They gathered together to talk about Blair House, and when Susan handed Alan the offering basket, he plunged his hand into his pocket. There was the quarter from last week and the quarter for this week, and Alan quickly gave them both.

Talk together: What did the story about Alan say to you? How is your offering used? Where does it go? What does it do?

Prayer: Dear Lord, you have given us so much. Help us share with others our love, our time, and our offering. Amen.

When Jesus Was A Little Boy
Matthew 11:16-19, 25-30

Brian was three years old. He liked coming to Sunday school and hearing stories about Jesus. "When Jesus was a little boy, was he in your class?" Brian interrupted his teacher's story.

Mrs. Anderson was telling the boys and girls a story about Baby Jesus who was born in a barn in Bethlehem. Brian liked that story and reminded his teacher, "I was a shepherd."

"Yes, I remember what you wore," she agreed.

"I had a towel around my head."

Beth added, "I was Mary."

Mrs. Anderson asked the children, "I wonder what Jesus liked when he was your age that made him happy?"

It was then Brian asked, "Was Jesus in your class when he was a little boy?" because Brian knew that being in Mrs. Anderson's class made him happy. He thought it would make Jesus happy, too.

Mrs. Anderson smiled. "Jesus lived a long, long, long time ago, Brian, so he was not in my class when he was a little boy." Brian was quiet. He looked sad. His teacher asked, "What is the matter, Brian?"

Brian replied, "I'm so sorry for Jesus that he couldn't be in your class!"

Talk together: In our Bible verses for today Jesus thanked God for revealing, showing, hidden, important things to infants, children (v. 25). Why did Brian tell his teacher he was sorry Jesus couldn't be in her class?

Prayer: Dear God, thank you for people who love and teach us the stories about Jesus and the stories Jesus told. Amen.

The Other Cheek
Matthew 5:38-39

There once was a boy who was always fighting. If someone accidently touched him, he hit them with his fist. If someone called him a funny name, he kicked them. If someone laughed at him, he beat up on them. After a while the others learned to fight back, and the boy came home lonely, with bruises and bad feelings.

One day someone asked, ducking his blow, "Why do you want to fight?"

"To show I am stronger than anyone else!" The boy clenched his fists.

"Does that make you feel good?" asked the other, as he ran.

The boy asked himself, "Does fighting make me feel good? Of course, winning is good. But winning is lonely."

The next time a child made a face at him, he began to beat up on him and the voice said, "Turn the other cheek." The boy turned his head the other way and continued hitting the other.

"No, silly, I mean if someone hits you on one cheek, turn the other, so he can hit that one, too."

The boy was so surprised by such a silly suggestion, he stopped fighting long enough to laugh. The more he thought about it, the harder he laughed. He laughed so loud the others heard him and began to laugh. Soon everyone was laughing, and it felt so good to be laughing *together* that the boy laughed even longer.

"This *is* better than fighting!" he thought. Since that day, whenever anyone calls him a funny name, he laughs, remembering the silly, but wise advice someone gave him long ago.

Talk together: Do you like to fight? Who said "Turn the other cheek. Forgive"?

Prayer: Dear God, help me remember Jesus' words when I am angry. Remind me to count to ten or laugh and "turn the other cheek." Amen.

If I Were The Church
Romans 12:4-5

Talk together:
"What is the church?" (*After the children have responded, stand and say*):
"If I were the church, my church bells would ring,"
(*Fold hands, place arms in front of body and swing them back and forth as "church bells."*)
"Come, everyone, I'd gladly sing."
(*Continue ringing "bells."*)
"If I were the church, I'd stretch my doors wide,"
(*Stretch arms to the side.*)
"And welcome everyone inside."
(*Close arms.*)
"If I were the church —"
"But I am you see,"
(*Point to yourself.*)
"For the church is people ... you, and you, and you,"
(*Point to others.*)
"And me."
(*Point to self.*)[1]

Invite the children to stand and say the words and do the motions with you.

If there is time and it is appropriate in your setting, ask the children to lead the congregation in standing and participating in the words and motions.

Prayer: Thank you, God, for the church. Amen.

_____

1. Elaine M. Ward, *Love in a Lunchbox* (Nashville, Tennessee: Abingdon Press, 1996), p. 83.

Coming To Church
Psalm 122:1

Carl liked to come to church. He liked to watch the people in white robes glide down the middle aisle, singing. His teacher called them the "choir."

When Reverend Rogers came by, Carl smiled and waved. He was the "minister" or "preacher" or "pastor." Like God, he had many names.

When everyone sat down, Carl saw the big box his mother called a "pulpit," and the big table his dad called an "altar."

On the side where his friend Sarah was sitting was a ... a ... Carl tried to remember. So many names. He turned the pages of the red book on his lap called a ... singbook, no, "hymnbook." And that bowl up front was a ... "baptismal font" where they put the water to baptize babies.

Carl whispered to his grandmother, pointing to the small, tall table that held the Bible, "What's that, Grandma?"

She answered briefly, "Lectern, Carl."

Grandma put out her hand, motioning for the red book, opened it, and stood up to sing. Carl remembered the time when they all sang a song he knew, "Jesus loves me, this I know...."

When the people sat down, the minister asked them all to pray with him. When he said, "Amen," he climbed into the box and began to talk. First he told a story.

Prayer: Dear God, we thank you for the church, the people, and the things that help us worship you. Amen.

To the Worship Leader: This story is to introduce the worship service. If most of the children are familiar, invite them to guess the words Carl is trying to learn.

Sharing
Luke 6:27-36

When the world was young, two brothers loved each other. Together they shared a field and a mill which they worked together. Each night they divided the grain they had ground that day and made sure the piles were even. One of the brothers was single and lived alone. The other brother was married and had a wife and children. One night the single brother said to himself and to God, "I have only myself to feed and my brother has a family to support. It is not fair that the grain is evenly divided." From that night on, he secretly took some of his grain to his brother's granary.

That same night the married brother said to himself and to God, "It is not fair that the grain is divided evenly. I have children who will provide for me in my old age and my brother has none." From that night on, he secretly took some of his grain to his brother's granary. To their surprise both brothers found their granaries mysteriously replenished.

One night the single brother took his grain to the granary later than usual and the married brother earlier than usual and the two met halfway between their granaries. When they realized what was happening, they embraced each other, thanking God for the peace "between them."

Talk together: Why did the brothers share? Why does the church ask us to share?

Prayer: Dear God, thank you for the love you have planted within our hearts. Help us listen to that voice within. Amen.

Habitat For Humanity
John 2:1-11

"Millard, what do you want to be when you grow up?"

Millard Fuller did not hesitate a moment to think but said immediately, "A millionaire!"

By the time he was thirty, he was a millionaire. He had a house in Palm Beach, California, another in Phoenix, Arizona, and an apartment in New York City, as well as boats and cars.

One day an old school friend came to visit Millard. "You must be the happiest man in the world. I have never eaten such fine food or seen such magnificent art."

Millard groaned. "It tastes like dirt to me. I have never been so unhappy."

The next day Millard sold his homes and boats and cars. He bought himself a small house and began to build homes for people who could not afford to buy them for themselves. He began an organization called Habitat for Humanity.

Soon people around the world joined him in building homes for "humanity." They built thousands of homes every year, gladly giving their time and work and money.

The next time Millard's school friend visited him, they recalled the boats and cars, the rich food and the art, and Millard told his friend, "I have never been happier. It is like changing water into wine," he said, sipping the refreshing ice cold water in his glass.

Talk together: Why was Millard unhappy? What did he do? What made him happy? What makes you happy?

Prayer: Dear Lord, create in us a happy heart and renew the spirit of joy within us. Amen.

This Little Light Of Mine
Matthew 5:13-20

(Bring a lamp that uses oil, such as in Jesus' time, and a basket.)

Jesus preached to the people. Once, sitting on a hillside, he said, "You are the light of the world. A city built on a hill cannot be hid. No one after lighting a lamp (*Light the lamp*) puts it under the bushel basket (*Put it under the basket*) but on a lampstand, and it gives light to all in the house. In the same way, let your light shine before others, so they may see your good works, and give glory to your Father in heaven."

Talk together: What do you think Jesus might have meant when he said, "You are the light of the world?" (*Pause*) Can we be plugged into electricity and shine? Jesus' words were for the people of the church who could see with their imagination. We call them "metaphors."

We sing a song about "this little light of mine," meaning the light our love casts.

This little light of mine, I'm going to let it shine.
This little light of mine, I'm going to let it shine.
This little light of mine, I'm going to let it shine.
Let it shine, let it shine, let it shine.
Everywhere I go ...
All through the night ...
(Substitute "anyone" for "Satan" in "Don't let Satan blow it out ... No ....")

Prayer: Dear Lord, let our lights shine, our words sing, and our prayers give you glory. Amen.

Francis Of Assisi
Genesis 1:31

Once upon a time there was a man named Francis who liked to play and sing and dance.

But in a dream he heard God say, "Repair (take care of) the place where I live."

Therefore, knowing God lives in the church, and the church where Francis lived was old and falling down, Francis began to build.

When the church was finished the people worshiped God there with great joy.

And God saw that it was good.

But Francis knew God was bigger than this one small church. Francis knew God lived in all the churches around the world, and at the head of the church, when Francis lived, was a pope, a man who cared more about himself than his people and the place where God lives.

Therefore, Francis began to repair (build up) the universal, the All-Church.

And God saw that it was good.

But Francis knew God was bigger than the All-Church. Francis knew God lived in, God's home was, the universe, the world. Francis' brothers and sisters were the sun and the stars, the sky and the seas, the birds and the beasts of the land.

Therefore, Francis began to take care of creation, to repair the place where God lives, for "the earth is the Lord's and all that is in it."

And God saw that it was good.

Therefore, we go in peace with Francis and God to care for the earth.

Talk together: What in creation makes you most glad?

Prayer: Lord, thank you. It is good! Amen.

The Aspen And The Wind
Mark 10:44

"Whoever wishes to be first must be servant of all."

James and John, friends of Jesus, said to him, "Teacher, we want you to do for us whatever we ask of you."

And Jesus said to them, "What is it you want me to do for you?"

They said to him, "Grant us to sit one at your right hand and one at your left in your glory."

They forgot to ask where the others would sit, and that reminds me of a story.

"Someday *I* will make beautiful music," said the small aspen tree, hearing the music float out of the tent. The aspen lived in the city of Aspen, Colorado, where beautiful music was made in the summer.

The old pine asked, "Who will teach you?"

"I need no teacher. I am tough and strong. I can do it alone."

The pine tree agreed, remembering the fire out of which the aspen grew through that adversity.

Day by day the small aspen grew tall and straight and sturdy. Listening to the music sweep through the streets and hills and skies of Aspen, he said, "Someday I *will* make music."

The spruce tree asked, "Who will help you sing?"

"I need no one. I am tough and strong. I can do it alone."

The spruce agreed, remembering the year there was no rain, yet the aspen grew through that adversity.

At the beginning of fall, the aspen's leaves turned golden and sparkled under the autumn sun. "Someday I will make *music!*"

The fir tree asked, "Who will help you sing before you lose your golden tones?"

"I need no help. I can do it alone."

But when the music school, the opera house, and the symphony hall closed and the music was leaving Aspen, the aspen cried.

"What is the matter?"

The aspen sobbed, "I cannot make music alone."

"The wind will help you."

The aspen asked the wind and the wind blew through its golden leaves, and there was music in the air, for at last the aspen had learned that we make music *together*.

Jesus said, "Whoever wishes to be first must be servant of all."

Talk together: What is the "music" you make? Do you do it alone or together with others?

Prayer: Dear Lord, thank you for wind, trees, music, things we sometimes take for granted. Help us learn to live with and create with others. Amen.

One Small Raindrop
Psalm 147:8

"God covers the sky with clouds; God supplies the earth with rain...."

Once there was a farmer who owned a large field of corn. He seeded and weeded it carefully, for when the corn grew, he would sell it, and buy food for his family. But no matter how hard he worked, the corn only withered and drooped, for there was no rain. "What will I do?" the farmer moaned, looking up at the sky and praying for rain. Two raindrops heard the farmer. One of them said, "I feel sorry for the farmer. I wish I could help him." The other said, "You are only a small raindrop. What can you do?"

"I cannot do much, it is true, but I can do what I can do. Here I go." The first raindrop began to fall. As the other raindrop watched, he said, "If you are going, I will go too. Here I come!"

The other raindrops gathered to see what was happening and cried together, "Let's go too!"

One after another the raindrops fell on the farmer's corn, and the corn grew and ripened, because one small raindrop did what it could do.

Talk together: What did the story say to you? What do you think God might want us to do?

Prayer: Dear God, open our eyes and ears, our hearts and minds to see what we can do and then to do it. Amen.

The Mustard Seed
Matthew 13:31-33, 44-52

(*Ask the children's choir or congregation to sing "Hymn of Promise" by Natalie Sleeth, #707,* The United Methodist Hymnal.)

Our story this morning is one that Jesus told, like a hymn of promise we just sang. Jesus said, "The kingdom of heaven is like a mustard seed, smallest of all the seeds, but inside is life that grows into a tree" (vv. 31-32 paraphrased).

(*Distribute mustard seeds or have an apple for cutting.*)

Alice asked, "How does life come from what we cannot see?"

Her mother said, "Bring me an apple." (*Cut open an apple to show the children.*) "What do you see?"

Alice said, "Small seeds."

Mother cut open a seed. "Now what do you see?"

Alice said, "Nothing!"

Mother replied, "We call growth that we cannot see God's gift of life, as the hymn said, 'In the bulb there is a flower, in the seed an apple tree, in the cold and snow of winter there is a spring that waits to be, a dawn in every darkness, in our death, a resurrection, God's victory!' We call the things we cannot see 'mysteries.' "

Talk together: Tell me something you know is there but you cannot see it. Talk about wind and love and God.

Prayer: Thank you, God, for mysteries that only you know, and thank you for seeds and trees and Jesus' stories. Amen.

Knowing God
Psalm 116:1-2 (GNB)

It was a new room for Zachary. It was his first Sunday in the three-year-old nursery. Zachary enjoyed playing with the other children, building churches and homes out of blocks, singing and moving with the music, and drawing with crayons until Mrs. Anderson said, "It's time for our juice and crackers."

The children sat in chairs gathered around a table. Zachary had been so busy playing, he forgot he was hungry.

Now he grabbed for his cracker.

Mrs. Anderson smiled. "Wait, Zachary. We are going to pray first."

Mrs. Anderson closed her eyes, lowered her head, folded her hands, and said, "Thank you, God, for food to eat. Amen."

Zachary sat on the edge of his chair, excited, as he cried, "My mommy knows God, too."

Talk together: How did Zachary know that Mrs. Anderson knew God? How do you know God? What is prayer for you?

Prayer: Thank you, God, for your love that helps us love others and ourselves, one of the ways we know you. Amen.

"Come And See"
John 1:29-42

When Jesus turned and saw two men following him, he said to them, "What are you looking for?" They asked him where he was staying and he said, "Come and see."

Once a teacher asked the children at church to draw a picture of God. But they had never seen God. Did God have hands and feet and eyes and ears the way we do? They sat quietly, thinking and feeling who God might be or how God might appear. Did God have wings as the angels? Did God fly like the clouds?

The paper was there. The crayons were there, and suddenly, an idea was there. Alan took the bright orange crayon and drew a circle, a large orange circle. Then he put down the crayon and thought again. With a yellow crayon he drew another circle, smaller and above the first. Then he drew eyes, a nose, and a mouth on each of them, and over all he drew a rainbow of many colors.

(*While telling, draw the circles and rainbow as they appear in the story.*)

When the children were asked to show their drawings, Alan held his picture before them and said, "Come and see. The sun is God the father, and the earth is the son, and the rainbow is the Holy Ghost, maybe!"

Talk together: What might you draw? Why did Alan end his description of his drawing of God with the word, "maybe"?

Prayer: Dear Lord, we know you are Spirit and Parent and Rock and Shepherd and Mystery, and although your name is important, even more important is that you are Creator and Love. May we love you always, whatever Your name. Amen.

All God Does, God Does Well
Luke 24:44-53

"The last time Jesus was with his friends, he lifted up his hands and blessed them, and was carried up into heaven. And they worshiped him and returned to Jerusalem with great joy...."

Some things we can't explain, and we call them mysteries and trust God's love no matter what. There is an old story about a rabbi taking a trip with his donkey, rooster, and lamp. When it was night, he had no place to sleep, so he slept in the woods. He lit his lamp to read his Bible before going to sleep, but a strong wind blew it over and broke it. "It must be time to sleep," the rabbi said, ending his prayers, "All God does, God does well."

During the night, in the dark, a wild animal came and frightened the rooster so that it ran away, and while the rabbi slept, thieves stole his donkey. When he awoke and saw what had happened, he said, "Well, well, well, all God does, God does well."

When it was time to return to his village, he learned that soldiers had come during the night, traveling through the woods, and killed all the people. If his lamp had not blown out, he would have been seen. If his rooster had not been chased away, it would have crowed, giving him away. If his donkey had not been stolen, it would have brayed. With great emphasis and joy once again the rabbi said, "All God does, God does well!"

Talk together: (*Fill a glass of water half full.*) There is a saying, "You can choose to see the glass half-empty or half-full." How do you see this glass?

Prayer: Dear God, thank you for mystery, things only you know, but help us remember that all you do, you do well, even when we do not understand. Amen.

71

Everywhere There Was God
John 4:5-42

One day Jesus stopped at a well where he asked a Samaritan woman for a drink of water. They talked together and Jesus told her many things. He said, "God is Spirit and those who worship God must worship in spirit and truth."

The students came to their teacher, asking, "Where is God?" The teacher smiled but did not answer their question. He wanted them to find their own answer for themselves, so he gave each of them a bird. "Go to a place where no one can see you and kill the bird." It seemed a strange and cruel order, but he was the teacher. At the end of the day the students returned with their dead birds. All but one of them. He told the teacher, "I set the bird free." The other students were shocked at his disobedience, and the teacher asked him to explain. "You told us to kill the bird in a place where no one would see us. I could not kill the bird because everywhere I went, there was God." And the teacher smiled.

Talk together: Everywhere Jesus went he taught about God. Can you remember anything Jesus taught or a story he told? (*Pause*) One of the things I remember is that God is Spirit; everywhere there is God.

Prayer: Dear God, we thank you for being with us wherever we are, and for Jesus' stories and words that help us live in your presence. Amen.

God Is Great, God Is Good
Psalm 106:1-6, 19-23

Every Sunday one of Betsy's parents drove into the circular drive of the church to deliver their child to church school. Sometimes Betsy stayed for worship, but her parents drove back home, because Sunday morning followed their wild Saturday night parties. Ambitious, upwardly-mobile people, it was part of the game — invite only the right people, all the way up to the boss. There were loud arguments and drunken laughter. One night Betsy awoke and came down the stairs. Seeing the eating and drinking, she said, "Oh, can I give the blessing? 'God is great, God is good, let us thank him for our food.' Goodnight, everybody." Betsy returned upstairs and suddenly the guests returned home. Mom and Dad faced each other over the empty glasses and dishes, and he said what they both were thinking, "Where do we think we are going?" The next morning Mr. and Mrs. Mom and Dad parked the car and during the worship service walked down the aisle to the front at the invitation to discipleship, to the banquet of their new "Boss."

Talk together: The psalm said, "Praise the Lord; give thanks for God's steadfast love." Who is your "Boss"? (*Accept children's answers from their "concrete" thinking.*) Who or what teaches us about God? How do you experience being with God?

Prayer: Dear God, we praise and thank you for your steadfast love. Amen.

God's Mercy
Psalm 51:1-17

The psalms (*Show the Psalms in the Bible.*) were the prayer poems of the people. The psalmist who wrote Psalm 51, wrote: "Have mercy on me, O God, according to your steadfast love; according to your abundant mercy blot out my transgressions."

"You are under arrest," the policeman said to the old man, caught for stealing a loaf of bread, because he was very hungry. The policeman brought the hungry man before the judge. "Your honor, this man has broken the law. He has been arrested for stealing." Now it happened that that night the mayor of the city, Fiorello La Guardia, was serving as judge in order to learn more about his people and their problems. The judge asked, "What did he steal?" "A loaf of bread." The judge fined the old man ten dollars, saying, "I am sorry but the law is the law. Stealing is against the law." Before he finished, the mayor reached into his pocket, took out his billfold, and paid the ten-dollar fine for the old man. Then he stood up and said to the people in the courtroom, "I am fining each of you fifty cents for living in a city that does not feed its hungry people." The mayor passed an empty plate among the people. When he had collected almost fifty dollars, he turned to the old man. "This money is yours to buy bread. You are free to go." The old man left the courtroom with tears in his eyes, for he had experienced God's mercy through God's people.

Talk together: Why was the man arrested? Have you ever done something wrong and were forgiven? That is God's "mercy."

Prayer: Dear God, we thank you for bread. Help us to share it with those who have no bread. Forgive us for living in a city that does not feed its hungry people. In Christ's name we pray. Amen.

God's Steadfast Love
Psalm 66:8-20

The psalmist sang of God's steadfast love: "Blessed be God, because God hears my prayer and gives me steadfast love" (v. 20 paraphrased).

One night a mother, praying with her daughter, asked her how she felt when she prayed. Her daughter answered, "It feels good because I feel good inside. I feel peaceful and happy." Her mother listened. Because her mother was listening, she continued, "Something else is filling me, but I don't know what to call it."

Her mother was quiet, now listening inside herself. Then she said, "Could it be God?"

Her daughter replied, "Maybe, because it's like we're connected and safe, as if God is touching me inside, gently ... It's as if we're hugging."

Talk together: Have you ever had the feeling that God is hugging you? How do you feel when you pray?

Prayer: Dear God, sometimes it's our parent's hug or the church's "hug" that feels as if you are hugging us, and we feel full inside and happy. Thank you. Amen.

Good Luck? Bad Luck? Who Knows?
Psalm 78:1-7

Jesus told parables, stories. Often he did not speak to them except in parable. Hear then the parable of "Good luck? Bad luck? Who knows?"

An old Chinese farmer had an old horse for tilling his fields. One day the horse ran away into the hills. The farmer's neighbors sympathized with the old man, saying, "Too bad. Bad luck."

The farmer replied, "Bad luck? Good luck? Who knows?"

A week later the horse returned with a herd of wild horses from the hills, and this time the neighbors said, "Good luck!"

His reply was, "Good luck? Bad luck? Who knows?"

Then, when the farmer's son was attempting to tame one of the wild horses, he fell off its back and broke his leg. The neighbors said, "Too bad. Bad luck."

The farmer said, "Bad luck? Good luck? Who knows?"

Some weeks later the army marched into the village and took every young man in good health. When they saw the farmer's son with his broken leg, they said, "Go home."

Now was that Good luck? Bad luck? or Who knows?

Talk together: What did this story say to you? How can you change bad luck to good luck? There is a story in the Bible of Joseph's brothers selling him into slavery, bad luck! But at the end God meant it for good, good luck!

Prayer: Dear Lord, help us accept what is and see the good within it, as you did in the Joseph story. Amen.

Have Mercy Upon Us!
Psalm 123

The two-year-old was visiting her grandparents, and as they gathered around the table, holding hands, they prayed a silent prayer before they passed the food. When they opened their eyes, the child joyously exclaimed, "Do it again!"

We held hands,
Said a silent prayer.
The Spirit was there.
And though only two
We knew she knew
When she said aloud,
"Do it again!"
Faith can't be taught.
Trust in God is caught
In hands held together,
In awe of the setting sun,
The moon and stars above,
God doing it again ...
And again ...
In mercy and in love.

Talk together: The psalmist prayed for mercy, God's love and grace, and as the young child said, we "do it again and again." When do you pray? Do you pray alone or with someone?

Prayer: Dear Lord, thank you for your love and presence. Help us remember to pray, again and again. Amen.

O Lord, Save My Life
Psalm 116:1-4, 12-19

There once was an eagle, a large, strong eagle who would stretch her wings and soar on the air.

(*Show a picture of an eagle.*)

One day she stopped soaring and was not seen for some time. The next time she took to the sky she carried on her back a baby bird, a small eaglet. Suddenly the eaglet fell. Down, down, down. It fell ... until it opened its tiny wings and flew.

However, its wings were weak and the wind was strong. The baby bird was tired and again it dropped faster and faster toward the ground, down, down, down ... until the mother eagle flew beneath her baby and caught it on her back. Then she soared higher into the sky for a second try.

Again she dropped the eaglet. Again it opened its wings to face the wind, and again it grew tired and began to drop, down, down, down ... but the mother was there.

So little by little, the eaglet learned to fly.

Talk together: In the Bible, the psalmist prayed, "O Lord, save my life," and the prophet Isaiah saw God as a mother who cares for and comforts her children. (*If boys say, "God is a man, not a 'mother,' " read Jesus' words in Matthew 23:37.*)

Prayer: Dear God, you are our Parent, Creator, Rock, and Mystery, who comforts and teaches us like a mother. We give you our praise and our thanks. Amen.

Only The Father Knows
Matthew 24:36-44

"... only the Father knows."

One day Sarah was sitting beside the window, looking out at the rain falling. Sarah was five and alive with curiosity, filled with questions and answers. "Rain is ..." Sarah said to her mother and brother, but then lost her words. "Mom, what are those runny, wet things from your eyes?"

Her mother replied, "Tears?"

"Yes. Rain is God's tears." Because it had been raining for four days, Sarah added, "This must be a sad month."

Sarah's brother, Charles, was seven. Listening, he said, "Sarah, I'm not sure rain is God's tears."

Listening to Charles, they waited, as he said, "I *know* the truth. I really do."

No one spoke. They watched the rain run down the window pane slowly as Charles spoke again, "I *think* I know the truth."

No one disagreed with Charles, and in the silence he spoke again, "*No one knows* the whole truth."

Jesus said something like that a long time ago, "Only the Father knows."

Talk together: Are there some things you think you know but you cannot prove? What do you think might have made Sarah think, "Rain is God's tears?" What might have made Charles say, "No one knows the whole truth."

Prayer: Dear God, we are glad for what we cannot see, such as the wind and love and you. We thank you and ask for love when we don't know "the whole truth." Amen.

The Blessing Of God
Psalm 133

The psalmist says that God gives good gifts. There is an old Jewish story that tells of two beggars, people who beg for their food in order to live. Each day the beggars came to the king, and he would give them bread. One of them praised and thanked the king. The other did not. Instead he prayed, "Thank you, God, for blessing the king so that he can help others." The king said to that beggar, "It is I who give to you, and you thank someone else." The beggar replied, "If God did not bless you, you could not bless others."

So the king told the baker, "Make two loaves of bread and put a priceless pearl in one of them to give to the beggar who praises me. Make the other loaf nothing but bread." The baker was very careful to do so.

The next day the beggar with the loaf of bread with the pearl said, "Thank you, O king, most generous of men!" But he noticed the loaf was heavy and badly baked, so he said, "Trade me, my good friend." Wanting to be helpful, the other took the bread. He found the pearl and prayed, "Thank you, God. Now I do not have to beg from the king."

The king was surprised when the man no longer came to beg and asked the baker what had happened. The baker said he had done exactly what the king had asked. So the king asked the beggar, "What did you do with the loaf the baker gave you?" "Ah, the loaf was hard, so I traded it with my friend."

Now the king understood that blessings come from God, for only God can turn a poor man into a rich man and even change the king's plan.

Talk together: What is a blessing God gives you? (Young children will not understand the following "moral.") Some things are "hard" to do but have a "reward" within them.

Prayer: Dear God, we thank you for the blessings of life and water, sunshine and fire, clean air and love. Amen.

The Glory Of God
Psalm 19

It was a new church for Sam. It was his grandmother's church, and because Sam loved his grandmother, he sat on the edge of the pew and tried hard to listen. "Are you saved?" the preacher asked from the pulpit far away. Sam remembered when he had saved pennies for a new plant for Mother on Mother's Day. "Maybe Mother saved pennies for me," Sam thought. The preacher continued, "Will you give your heart to Jesus?" Sam wondered where his heart was. But if Jesus needed Sam's heart he would be glad to give it. Sam whispered, "Grandma, do I have a ..." "Shhh, Sam, you are in church." "Take Jesus as your Savior ..." the minister continued. Sam wondered where he was to take Jesus. Sam had a lot of questions to ask his grandmother. "Will you come forward ..." Sam was sitting at the front of the church. He turned around, waiting for the others to come. "... to make a profession ..." "What's a prof...?" "Shhh, Sam!" Grandmother sighed! "... and commit your life ..." Sam knew better than to ask his grandmother what "commit" meant, "... to be baptized, forgiven, redeemed...?" Sam smiled. He knew what baptize meant, but the other words were new words. Sam leaned back against the pew and looked out of the windows. It was warm and Sam was becoming sleepy. Maybe someday he would understand what the minister was saying, but for now he pretended he was outside listening to the birds and counting the clouds in the heavens that were telling the glory of God.

Talk together: The psalmist said that the heavens tell us of the glory of God. How do you know and experience "the glory of God"?

Prayer: Dear Lord, we thank you for heaven and earth, for they are yours and everything in them. Amen.

Trinity Sunday
Matthew 28:16-20

(Read the text aloud.)

My granddaughter knows the meaning of Trinity.
She is Amber, Lisa, Tiger Lily, all three,
For as she said, trying to explain,
"All three are one in me."

A bishop pointed to the figure of Christ being baptized in the River Jordan pictured in a stained glass window and asked the children gathered at the altar, "Is this God?" They answered, "Yes."

He pointed to the Holy Spirit in the form of a dove hovering over the head of Christ. "And is this God?" They answered, "Yes." He then pointed to the Father in the clouds, "Is this God?" They answered, "Yes."

"But," he asked, "that makes three gods?"

One of the children quickly replied, "No, one god."

The bishop mused, "But I do not understand," to which the boy replied, "You are not supposed to understand. It's a mystery!"

Talk together: Are there things you don't understand? What do you do? Jesus commanded his disciples to obey and remember that he is with them always.

Prayer: Dear God, the three-in-one, we worship you in mystery because you are God. Help us to love when we do not understand. In Christ's name. Amen.

The Monkey Who Wanted Misery
Romans 8:26a

Talk together: What is "misery"? What is the very worst thing that might happen to you?

A storyteller and author, Diane Wolkstein, went to Haiti and collected 27 stories, which Schocken published in a book called *The Magic Orange Tree and Other Haitian Folktales*, 1997 (www.dianewolkstein.com). I will tell it in dialect.

Monkey, sitting in tree, when woman on her way to market, trip on vine and calabash on her head fall to the ground and break in a thousand pieces and the sweet syrup ran all over the ground. "Oh, Papa God, what Misery you have given me. For three days I walk to market to sell sticky sweet syrup, and now look! What Misery!" But there was nothing she could do, so woman go on her way.

Monkey, being curious, come down from tree and sniff sticky sweet syrup and it smell good. He taste sticky sweet syrup and it taste good. He lick up all the sticky sweet syrup and Monkey want more. So Monkey find Papa God.

"Papa God, Papa God," Monkey cry.

"Good morning, Monkey," say Papa God.

"I have come to see you, Papa God."

"Yes, Brother Monkey."

"I come to ask ..."

"Yes, Monkey?"

"I come to ask for ... Misery!"

"Monkey, in your condition you want Misery?"

"I have tasted Misery and it is sweet and I want lots and lots of Misery."

Papa God get strange requests, but he say, "You see that sack by the tree. Bring it here. Now if you want Misery, lots of Misery, put the sack on your back and walk and walk and walk until there are no trees."

83

"Yes, Papa God!"

Monkey took sack and put on back and walk and walk and ... walk ... until there are no trees. He put down sack and can almost taste the sticky sweet syrup. He loosened string and open and grrr, grrr, five big dogs jump out of sack and chase Monkey. Monkey ran and ran and ran, but there were no trees. The dogs growled and were almost on Monkey. Suddenly there was one tree and Monkey climb tree and dogs growl and snarl, but they cannot get Monkey.

Papa God send one tree. For Papa God know too much Misery is not good for anyone, not even Monkey.[1]

Prayer: Thank you, God, for your Spirit that is sweet as honey. Help us learn how to pray. Amen.

---

1. Diane Wolkstein, *The Magic Orange Tree and Other Haitian Folktales* (New York: Shocken, 1997). Used by permission.

All Saints' Day
Matthew 5:1-12

A young boy, reading about the saints, decided to become one. He picked a model and began to imitate him. The model he picked was Simon Stilotes who lived on a big pillar in the middle of the town square. The boy did not have a pillar, so he placed a chair in the kitchen and stood on it. His mother came in the back door and nearly knocked him over. He moved, but his sister needed to get to the sink, so he moved again. But his brother opened the refrigerator door and the chair slid. He moved again just as his father walked into the kitchen and knocked him from the chair. Picking up the chair, he walked out the door, muttering to himself, "It's just not possible to be a saint at home!"

Talk together: Jesus preached a sermon about being "saints." It is called the "Beatitudes." What is a "saint"? Someone once said that a saint is someone who lets the light of God shine through. Have you ever tried, as the boy in the story, to be a "saint"?

Prayer: Thank you, God, for helping us to try to be "saints," that is, to love one another, forgiving us and loving us just as we are. Amen.

Baptism
Matthew 3:13-17

In our Bible story Jesus went to John the Baptist at the River Jordan to be baptized. In those days people were baptized by walking into the water and being dunked. And when Jesus had been baptized, just as he came up out of the water, suddenly a voice from heaven said, "This is my beloved Son, with whom I am well pleased."

Jennifer was six and her greatest joy was to go with her father on his trips. He enjoyed the company of his daughter, as well. As a preacher, one day he invited Jennifer to go with him to another city where he would be preaching and she said, "Yes!" In the car he decided to talk to Jennifer about his sermon and asked, "Where do you think God is?" After thinking a moment, she said, "Well, God is in heaven." Her father decided to push her a bit and said, "But, Jennifer, people have looked up into the sky with powerful telescopes and in spaceships and have never seen God." Jennifer thought some more and said slowly, a bit upset, "Well, God is in your heart then." Jennifer's father forgot that God is Spirit and you don't see God with your eyes and said, "But, Jennifer, people have opened hearts and have never found God there either." Jennifer began to cry and her father felt badly, when suddenly she continued, "Well, all I know, Daddy, is that God was what I knew before I knew anything else." Jennifer's tears and words were like a baptism, when out of the heavens, whether from the sky or from his heart, her father heard the words, "This is my beloved daughter. Listen to her."

Talk together: How does God speak? What might be some ways?

Prayer: Dear God, whether in heaven or our hearts, we know you before we know anything else. Thank you for being like a loving Parent, loving and listening to us always. Amen.

During Lent
Psalm 116:12-19

In the classroom Bernadette prayed that the floor would open so she could fall in it, or if not that, have wings to fly and disappear. Instead her teacher said, "Bernadette, you will stay until you have learned your prayer." It was the teacher's job to teach the children to pray. Bernadette was supposed to have memorized her prayer, that is, say it without looking at the words, but there was so much to do at home, she had not had the time. Mother was ill so she had to milk the cow, feed the baby, sweep the floor, and then at the last minute, run out of the room to school.

The monk, the teacher, sat in his office, praying, "God, help me to teach the children to pray." He was still praying when Bernadette knocked on his door. "I know my prayer," she said, crossing her arms over her chest in the form of praying. (*Do.*) Then she saw the loaf of bread, and the monk asked, "Have you eaten today?"

Bernadette shook her head, and the monk gave her half of his loaf. As she ate, she again crossed her arms and began to pray. (*Do.*) The monk suddenly stood up and cried, "That's it! Bernadette, I will listen to your prayers tomorrow!"

The next morning the monk said to the children, "I have a *pretiola* for you," using the Latin word for "little present." As each said their prayer, the monk handed them bread twisted in the shape of praying. (*Do.*) It was a pretzel, and now today, during Lent, we remember to pray, as we make and eat pretzels.

Talk together: Give each child a small pretzel, saying, as you cross your arms on your chest, "Let us now pray as Bernadette did."

Prayer: During Lent, dear God, we thank you for your love, for food and health and people who pray and care for us. Amen.

Passion/Palm Sunday
Matthew 21:1-11

"Hosanna!" the people cried. "Hosanna! Save us!"

As God heard the shouting, God saw Jesus approaching the people, riding on the back of a small donkey. God watched and listened, for the people were excited. So were the disciples. "Lord, look how the people love you. They want you to be their king! We will be famous and important!"

Jesus shook his head. "See what I am riding? Is there a more humble animal? Look, I have no sword nor crown."

The people cheered more loudly. They waved palm branches and threw their coats on the road. "But, Jesus, the people need ..."

God listened. What would Jesus answer?

Jesus was silent, waiting to hear his disciples tell him what the people needed. Then God heard Jesus tell his friends what the people needed and who he was, "The people need ... a suffering servant."

God smiled, for it was good.

Distribute palm branches for the children to wave as you say the words:

Jesus is coming!
He's coming today!
Hosanna! Hosanna!
Hip! Hip! Hurrah!

He's coming to bless us,
To teach us God's way,
Hosanna! Hosanna!
Hip! Hip! Hurrah!

Talk together: Why are we celebrating today?

Prayer: Dear Lord, thank you for Jesus, and his words and actions. Help us to love and honor him. Amen.

Pentecost
Acts 2:1-21

One day Jesus' friends came together. They were sad because Jesus was no longer with them. They missed Jesus, but suddenly there was a loud noise that sounded like the flapping of many wings and everyone covered their ears. They saw what seemed to be tongues of fire rest on the heads of each of them, and they were filled with God's Spirit. They spoke, but in different languages. They knelt on the floor and thanked God for God's love and presence. They told the story of Jesus around the world, for that was the day the church was born.

There was once a man who loved God. Because he loved God, he loved other people. One day he met a sick man who needed medicine and a doctor and a place where he could get well. The man said, "I will build a hospital. But I cannot build a hospital alone. I need others who will help me." The man found other people who loved God. Because they loved God, they loved others, too. Together they built a hospital. Together they bought medicine. Together they paid the doctors and the nurses who cared for the sick. There were many things the man could do alone to show his love. There were many things he needed others to help him do. The church is like that, people who love God and serve and help others alone and together.

Talk together: At Pentecost we gather together in the church. What do you like best about our church?

Prayer: When we are afraid, God, remind us of your church, the gathering place where we love and worship you, and where we are loved, too. Amen.

89

Jesus At Twelve
Luke 2:41-52

Mary said to Joseph, "I thought Jesus was with you!" Joseph replied, "I thought Jesus was with you." Mary and Joseph asked among the party in which they were traveling if anyone had seen Jesus, their son. Benjamin said, "The last time I saw him he was still in Jerusalem in the Temple." Quickly Mary and Joseph returned to the City where only three days before they had celebrated the Festival of the Passover. To everyone they passed on the way to the Temple, they asked about Jesus. "How old is he?" the strangers asked. Joseph replied, "He is twelve." At last they elbowed their way into the temple chambers where the teachers were and, to their surprise, listened to Jesus' questions and replies. Mary interrupted, "Jesus, what are you doing? We have been worried." Jesus looked up at his parents and smiled. "Why were you searching for me? Did you not know I would be in my Father's house?" Gently Joseph put his arm around Jesus' shoulder. "It is time to leave." Together Mary, Joseph, and Jesus returned to Nazareth where Jesus continued to ask questions that would help him know God's will and way.

Talk together: What does this story say to you? What would you like to know about God?

Prayer: Dear Lord, I am glad for Jesus' example of asking questions about your will and your way. Let me not think I understand your mystery so completely that I do not continue to seek and grow in knowledge and experience of your presence. Amen.

Jesus And The Children
Luke 18:15-17

Pantomime "Jesus And The Children" while it is being read. Characters are Jesus, disciples, parents, and children. Assign children to these parts. Do the italicized motions:

As the children *walked* along the way, they saw the flowers blooming, the birds singing, and Jesus on the hill. Some began to *run*. Some *skipped*. Some *walked slowly* beside their mothers and fathers. When they reached the hill, they saw many people, but they could not see Jesus because there were too many people. They *stood on their tiptoes*. They *made themselves small* and squeezed through the crowd. But Jesus' friends *stopped them*, saying, "Jesus is too busy." The children *were sad*. They *stopped* and *turned around*. Then they *heard* him say, "Let the children come to me!" The children *ran* to Jesus and began to *sing*.

Talk together: Ask the "children": How did you feel when the disciples stopped you?

Ask the "parents": How did you feel when the disciples stopped your children?

Ask the "disciples": How did you feel when Jesus reversed your actions?

Ask "Jesus": How did you feel when the disciples said you were too busy to see children?

Follow through with "Why?"

Prayer: Dear Lord, thank you for loving us, and for people who protect and guide us. Be with us always. Amen.

The Good Samaritan ... But ...
Luke 10:25-37

Jesus told stories because people like, listen to, and remember stories. He once told a story about a friend. Friends are important. This is the story Jesus told:

A man set out from home, and as he was walking, robbers came and beat him up and stole what he had. They left him beside the road to die.

But someone came along, saw the hurt man and ... quickly passed by. He was afraid he might be blamed for hurting the man or sued for helping him. Besides, the man was bleeding and he was supposed to stay clean.

But another man came along. He was in a hurry, however, and didn't have time to stop.

But a stranger, a Samaritan, came by. He saw the hurt man.

But he was his enemy.

But he stopped.

He cleaned the wounds, bandaged them, put the hurt man on his donkey, and took him to a place where he would be cared for. He paid the innkeeper and promised to pay more when he returned.

When Jesus ended the story, he asked, "Which man was the friend?"

I have named the story of the Good Samaritan, "BUT!"

But I would like to reframe it for you.

A girl came into a new classroom. She had just moved to town and was a stranger. She was lonely and needed a friend. Her name was Beth.

When Alice entered the room Beth smiled at her, *but* Alice was in a hurry to talk with Susan and pretended she did not see Beth.

But Bill entered next. He glanced at Beth, saw she was a stranger, *but* a girl, and quickly crossed the room to the other side.

92

But ... "Hi, James," Bill called across the room, as James entered.

James saw Beth. He saw a stranger who needed a friend. "Hi, my name is James. What is your name?"

Which one is the friend?

Talk together: In both stories, which one was the friend? Has anyone ever treated you the way the "good Samaritan" did, or the way James did?

Prayer: Dear Lord, we thank you that there are people who care, brave and faithful, knowing your love and compassion and will. Amen.

The Three Trees
Psalm 1:3

Choose four volunteers — a narrator and three trees to do a readers' theatre of "The Three Trees."

Narrator: Three trees lived on a high hill, overlooking the sea and each of them had a dream.

First Tree (1): I want to be a box one day that will hold the greatest treasure in the world.

Second Tree (2): I want to be a sailing ship and carry the greatest king of the world.

Third Tree (3): I want to grow tall so that all the people may see me point to God.

Narrator: And the trees grew and grew and grew until one day men came up the hill and cut down the trees.

1: Oh, dear, look what I have become! Not a box to hold the greatest treasure in the world, but a box for hay for the horses and cows.

2: Look at me. I am simply a poor rowboat that carries smelly fish and fishermen, not the greatest king of the world.

3: At least the two of you are something. I am simply a useless plant of wood that will never be lifted up to point to God.

Narrator: And the days and months and years passed, and one dark night a mother placed her newborn baby in the manger that held the hay for the animals.

l: Look! Look! I am holding the greatest treasure in the world!

Narrator: And the days and months and years passed, and one dark night a terrible storm arose and the fishermen were very afraid and the man called Jesus stood up in the boat and said, "Peace," and the water was still.

2: Look! Look! I am carrying the greatest king in the world across the sea!

Narrator: And the days and months and years passed, and one dark night the man called Jesus was hung on a cruel cross made from the useless plant of wood.

3: Look! Look! From now on when anyone looks at me, they will point to God and remember God's great love in the man called Jesus who God raised from the dead on Easter!

Talk together: Did the three trees' wishes come true? What did the first wish? The second? The third?

Prayer: Dear God, help us trust your plan and promise which is more important than that for which we pray. Amen.

The Two Sons
Matthew 21:23-32

Jesus said, "A father had two sons, two boys (*Young children sometimes confuse their "suns"*). Early one morning the father asked the first son to help him, and the son said, "No, sorry, Dad!" The father asked the second son to help him. The second son said, "Yeah! Sure!"

Now the sun in the sky began to move across the day, and the son who had said, "No," changed his mind and went to help his father. The second son, who had said, "Yes," found something else to do and forgot his promise to his father.

Jesus asked the people who were listening, "Which of the two did the will of his father?"

Later, another rabbi (storyteller) asked those who were listening, "What would you do if you were walking along and found a purse full of money lying on the street?" The first said, "I would return it to its owner." The rabbi thought, "Perhaps he answers too quickly. Does he mean what he says?" The second student said, "I would keep it, if no one saw me," and the rabbi thought, "That's deceitful." The third answerer said, "To be honest, I would be tempted to keep it. So I would pray to God to give me the strength to do the right thing." The rabbi said to the people, "Go and do the same."

Talk together: Have you ever said, "No," and changed your mind? Why do you think the first son changed his mind?

Prayer: Dear God, help us to say, "Your will be done," and listen for your will for us. Give us strength to say, "Yes," to you and do it. Amen.

The Great Commandment
Matthew 22:34-46

In our Bible story for today someone asked Jesus which commandment was the greatest. He said to him, " 'You shall love the Lord your God with all your heart, and with all your soul, and with all your mind.' This is the greatest and first commandment. And a second is like it: 'You shall love your neighbor as yourself.' "

That love comes from God. Jesus called God the "good shepherd."

There was a good shepherd with a flock full of sheep
Who took them to pasture where they could eat.
He watched them through day and he watched them through
    sleep.
But one was mischievous and wandered away,
So he gathered the others and told them to stay.
And all through the nighttime he searched and he searched.
Then he prayed, "Dear God of the lonely, the least and the
    lost,
Help me remember and not count the cost,
To love and look after the sheep that has strayed."
And all through the night the good shepherd prayed.
Then with the daylight the good shepherd found
The little, lost lamb, his foot caught under a rock,
And rejoicing, returned the lost lamb to the flock.
Sometimes I'm like that lost lamb too,
Scared or lonely and don't know what to do.
Then God, the Good Shepherd, calls out to me,
And rejoicing, returns me to God's family.

Talk together: After poetry, sometimes we are silent and simply pray.

Prayer: Dear Shepherd, find me and fill me with love so I may love others, as you love me. Amen.

Zacchaeus
Luke 19:1-10

"It's not fair! I wish I weren't so small," sighed Zacchaeus. Zacchaeus had always been small. As he and his friends grew, he was different from the rest. "It's not fair! I'll show them!" Because Zacchaeus felt left out, he was angry. He decided he would get even with them! When he became older, he became a tax collector and cheated the people, taking more of their money for himself.

"It's not fair!" said the people. "Zacchaeus is taking more than is required as a tax collector." One day the people were gathered in the village square because they had heard that Jesus was coming to their village. Because Zacchaeus was small, he could not see. "It's not fair!" said Zacchaeus, standing on tiptoes among the crowd. So Zacchaeus climbed a tree, and when Jesus came, he said to him, "Zacchaeus, come down. I am going to your house today!"

"It's not fair!" grumbled the crowd. "Why would Jesus eat with Zacchaeus? He is a cheater!" The crowd stood outside the house when Jesus went inside. They stayed there until the door was opened and Zacchaeus and Jesus came out. "People of the village," said Zacchaeus. He smiled at Jesus. "I return to you four times what I have taken from you. Please forgive me, as God has forgiven me." The people nodded their heads, smiling at Jesus to thank him. Then Jesus began to teach them of God's plan when things "are not fair."

Talk together: With whom do you identify in this story? Zacchaeus, the people, or Jesus? Why do you think Jesus ate with Zacchaeus?

Prayer: Dear Lord, forgive us as Jesus did Zacchaeus, and help us respond as Zacchaeus and Jesus did. Amen.

All Kinds Of Doubts
Mark 9:24

A father came to Jesus with his son who needed healing. He begged Jesus, "Help us!"

Jesus said, "If you are able! — All things can be done for the one who believes."

Immediately the father cried, "I believe; help my unbelief!"

Talk together: Have you ever read the story *Wrinkle in Time*? The author Madeleine L'Engle's married name was Madeleine Franklin. One day, as she was teaching a writing workshop, one of her students asked, "Mrs. Franklin, do you really and truly believe in God with no doubts at all?"

Mrs. Franklin smiled. "Oh, Una, I really and truly believe in God with all kinds of doubts, and I base my life on this belief."

What can you tell me about trust and believing? About your experience with prayer?

Prayer: Lord, we believe, sometimes with "all sorts of doubts." Help us live out of our belief and trust in you. Amen.

The Seed
Mark 4:1-9

There once was a seed and in that seed was life. The seed was buried in the earth. In the dark, wet ground it waited. It waited and waited. At the right time, the seed burst through its shell to search for the sun. In order to grow, the seed needed the sun. But something held it within the ground. If the seed could have seen up above, it would have seen a heavy, moss-covered log lying on its birthplace. The seed could not live without light from the sun. But the log prevented it from growing tall and straight. The seed, feeling life within, searched for another way to find the light.

One day a little girl cried, "Look! A leaf!" Her mother came and saw the log. She pushed aside the log to see the crumpled daffodil, twisted and bent, hugging the ground. Now, without the log covering it, the daffodil grew, for all life needs light and food and love.

Talk together: What did the story say to you? What is your favorite story in the Bible? What is your favorite story?

If you are using these stories in a church school setting, plant seeds and watch them grow.

Think of a "seed" in your life, something just beginning, be it your trust in God, a relationship with a new friend, a hobby, or a new idea.

Think of the seed of growth of life. Imagine Jesus giving out seeds. He turns, smiles, and gives one to you, saying, "Now go with God and plant your seed." You decide where to plant your seed and watch it grow. As it grows what does it represent to you in your life right now? What stage is it in? Talk with your seed. See it in full bloom.

Draw your seed in whatever image you see it and its growth.

Prayer: Dear God, we thank you for seed and growth, for rain and sunshine, and especially for your love. Amen.

The House On The Rock
Matthew 7:24-27

Jesus told a story about a man who built his house upon a rock and another man who built his house upon the sand, and when the winds blew and the rain fell, the house on the rock stood strong, but the house on the sand fell down.

I think of the three little pigs. When it was time for them to build their own homes, the first pig met a man with straw and bought it and built a house. As soon as he had, the wolf came by. "Little pig, little pig, let me come in." "Not by the hair of my chinny chin chin." "Then I'll huff and I'll puff and I'll blow your house in." And because the little pig's house was built out of straw, the wolf blew it in and the little pig ran away and hid.

The second little pig met a man with a bundle of sticks and the little pig bought them and built a house. As soon as he had, the wolf came by. "Little pig, little pig, let me come in." "Not by the hair of my chinny chin chin." "Then I'll huff and I'll puff and I'll blow your house in." And because the little pig's house was built out of sticks, the wolf blew it in and the little pig ran away and hid.

The third little pig met a man with bricks and the little pig purchased them and built himself a house on rock. As soon as he had, the wolf came by. "Little pig, little pig, let me come in." "Not by the hair of my chinny chin chin." "Then I'll huff and I'll puff and I'll blow your house in." The wolf huffed and puffed, but because the pig's house was built on rock, the wolf blew himself "in," and the others came out from hiding to live with their brother, happily ever after *on the rock.*

Prayer: Dear God, you are my rock and my fortress, keeping me safe. Thank you for your everlasting love. Amen.

The Loving Father
Luke 15:11-32

"Alan, you are late again!" Alan's father's jaw twitched, which meant Alan's father was not pleased. Alan's father was angry. "This is the third time this week you have been late to dinner!" The family was seated at the dinner table when Alan slammed the door, dropped his books on the floor, pulled out his chair, and sat down at the table. "I'm sorry. I didn't know what time it was." It was Alan's usual excuse.

The next morning at the breakfast table there was a surprise package beside Alan's plate. Alan unwrapped the package. It was an inexpensive watch, but it was Alan's. He grinned. "Now I don't have an excuse."

That evening the family was sitting at the dinner table when Alan slammed the door, dropped his books on the floor, pulled out his chair, and sat down at the table. "I'm sorry. I forgot to watch the time." Father glared at Alan across the table, his jaw twitching, which meant Alan's father was angry. "If you are late tomorrow, your dinner will be bread and water!"

The next night dinner was later than usual. "Mary, what is slowing up dinner?" Father asked. Mother said nothing, simply setting the table, seeing Alan's empty chair. When everyone was at last seated at the dinner table, their plates filled with food, Alan slammed the door, dropped his books on the floor, pulled out his chair, and sat down at the table. "I'm sorry ..." Alan looked down at his plate with a piece of dry bread and a glass of water and remembered. Everyone was eating fried chicken, mashed potatoes and gravy, and crisp orange carrots, his favorite foods. His stomach growled with hunger and he coughed so no one would hear it. He wanted to hold his nose so he wouldn't smell the fried chicken. Then a tear rolled down Alan's cheek. Everyone continued to eat. No one paid any attention to Alan until his father reached out, took Alan's empty plate and glass of water and gave Alan his plate of fried chicken, mashed potatoes, crisp orange carrots, and glass of milk.

That night Alan's father went to bed hungry and Alan never forgot that meal, for as he told his children years later, "All my life I have known what God is like because of what my father did that night."

Talk together: How do you know God is like a loving Parent? Do you have a "father like that"? Jesus told a story of a "father like that."

Prayer: Thank you, God, for being our loving Parent.

Jesus' Resurrection
Mark 16:6

The small, furry, green caterpillar ate its way up the stalk of grass. Slowly, silently it munched its way. The man on the hill watched the caterpillar. For the first time that day he was alone. The man sat silently thinking and watching the caterpillar. What was he thinking as he watched the caterpillar, this strong, silent man? Who was he? From where had he come? Like the caterpillar, where was he going? What was he meant to do? These were the man's thoughts as he sat watching the caterpillar eat, doing what the caterpillar was meant to do.

Some people live quietly, seeking God's will. This man was impatient. Ever since his baptism by John he had asked God what he must do. As he watched the caterpillar eat, he remembered that soon it would spin its cocoon and die. This was why it was eating the green leaves. Then the man knew. He knew what he would do. Slowly, he rose and left the hill.

The city was crowded with people because it was a great holiday. There was much to see and do. The people went to the temple and to the marketplace. Some of the people even went to the hill where the criminals were hung on heavy, rough crosses. This year there would be three of them. This year the people who visited the hill were especially curious, for one of the criminals to be hung was the loving, rebel preacher, the carpenter from Nazareth.

The people shouted when they saw him dragging his cross behind him. "Save yourself, preacher! Remember, you are God's son!" they mocked. The man did not reply. He had come to die. Soon it would be over. He remembered the last time he had been on that hill, watching the small caterpillar doing what it must do, the day he had decided to do what he must do. Today there was no caterpillar to watch. Today he was dragging a cross on which he would die. The man, however, was not afraid. He was not bitter or discouraged, for he knew that God was with him. That day the man died on the hill called Calvary.

Later that night they took his body from the cross and wrapped it like a cocoon in soft white sheets and put it in a tomb. A few days later, when a friend of the man went to the tomb, the white sheets lay on the ground, for the man's body was no longer there. The woman wondered and began to cry. "Why are you crying?" asked a voice behind her. The woman turned, for she thought she recognized the voice. She thought she recognized the man, but he was different, and on his shoulder rested a small, white butterfly.

Talk together: Do you have any questions about this story? It is one of the most important stories for us, who call ourselves "Christians."

Prayer: Dear God, we thank you for Christ and his sacrifice and for your power to raise us from the dead now and yet to come. Amen.

Transfiguration Sunday
Matthew 17:1-9

Leader, wearing dark glasses, asks the children, "Do you know why I am wearing dark glasses?" (*Pause*)

The Bible story for today says that Jesus took his friends Peter, James, and John up a mountain to pray. While they were praying, Jesus' face changed and his clothes became dazzling white, so bright it blinded their eyes. Then two men appeared, Moses and Elijah, and they began talking with Jesus about what would happen when Jesus went to Jerusalem. Suddenly a cloud came and covered them, and a voice said, "This is my Son, my Chosen. Listen to him." When they came down from the mountain, everything was "tranfigured."

Talk together: If you saw Jesus in white robes coming down our center aisle to sit on the steps with us, what would you do? (*Pause*) Some of us might close our eyes, thinking this is too good to be true. Jesus here?

In what way might Jesus be here with us right now? One of the ways is to use our faith imagination. Close your eyes. We are walking toward the hill where we can be alone. The sky is blue, the flowers are blooming, the birds are singing, and when we reach the hillside we sit down and invite Jesus to be with us. Suddenly he is there in bright, white robes. We are silent and feel the light breeze blow. A voice says, "This is my Son. Listen to him." We listen and Jesus speaks to us. (*Pause*) Then we do what we need to do and return to this place, knowing we can be with Jesus in our faith imagination whenever we wish. Now open your eyes.

Prayer: Dear God, thank you for hearts to love, minds to think, and faith imagination to know your presence here and now, among us. Amen.

Ask Me, I Will Do It
John 14:1-14

Brad was a good student. He studied hard because he enjoyed learning, but when he was sick, he did not enjoy anything. "Brad, you will be better tomorrow," his mother assured him, smoothing his pillow. "I called Mrs. Adams and she understands." Brad tried to smile, but his stomachache would not let him. The next morning, however, Brad felt fine, just as his mother had said. But when Brad arrived in his school room, there was a substitute teacher. "Now what?" Brad thought. "This teacher will not know I was sick yesterday."

Ms. Jones said, "Boys and girls, we will go around the room to give everyone a chance to do a math problem based on what Mrs. Adams taught you yesterday, according to her note to me." Brad's stomachache began to hurt again. He listened to Adam and Alice and Jeff and Ginny and knew it was his turn next. "God, help me," he prayed silently. Ms. Jones called, "Philip." She had skipped Brad! After class Ms. Jones called to Brad, "Let me help. Ask me and I will do it." And she did. Brad's prayer was answered.

Talk together: Have you ever prayed for something and it happened? Have you ever prayed and it did not happen? God is not a magician to do our work for us, but God will help us work.

Prayer: Dear God, help us be brave when we are afraid and loving when it is difficult. We pray to you for the things you can do and we work at the things we can do. In Christ's name. Amen.

Listening
Mark 1:35

Jesus was a healer. Because he was a healer he was a pray-er, for he knew his power to heal came from God. Once after he had been praying, one of his friends said, "Lord, teach us to pray."

Molly began to pray when she was very young. She felt close to God when she prayed. Each night she asked God to bless and take care of her family and friends.

She said, "Thank you, God, it was a good day today." Sometimes in Sunday school or church or just walking along, she sang her praise.

Sometimes, at night, when it was dark and she was in bed, alone, she remembered how she had made fun of her best friend, Susan, and Susan cried. Molly told God she was sorry.

Sometimes she told God she was afraid and asked for courage. Sometimes she was confused and asked God to send her a good idea. Prayer was the way she related to God.

But one day, when she was ten years old, she stomped into the kitchen, shouting, "If God won't talk to me, then I won't talk to God." Her father put down his newspaper to listen.

Molly wanted to hear God speak in words, in English! "If there is nothing I can hear or see or touch or taste, how do I know God is real?"

When Molly had put her feelings into words, she felt better. She asked her father, "Does God talk to you?" He replied, "When I was your age, I used to climb a tree in our backyard to talk with God, thinking I would be closer to heaven. I looked at creation as one of the ways God 'speaks.' When I grew older, I learned God is Spirit and is heard with the heart and we are touched with the spirit. God 'speaks' in many different ways. One day I even wrote a poem:

"I keep listening for God,
Thinking God will speak
With words we use,
Rather than burning bushes,
    white-winged doves,
    and angel messages in dreams.
I keep listening for God,
Thinking God will speak
With words we use
Rather than songs of sparrows,
    sprouting seeds,
    hugs and handshakes,
Rather than dance,
    dinner with loved ones,
    and praying with faith imagination.
I keep thinking I'll turn a corner
    and God will be there,
    handing me a hand-written letter
    or one blazed across the sky.
I keep listening for God to speak to me,
And in the silence I feel God's love."

Talk together: Have you ever felt like Molly? How does God "speak" to you? How do you know God is with you? What were the ways the writer of the poem thought God might speak?

Prayer: God, thank you for your presence in creation, in people, in prayer and story and song, especially in Jesus, the Christ. Amen.

Intercession
Matthew 5:43-48

There was once a man who dreamed of a beautiful home, and soon all of his time, energy, money, and attention were devoted to building his home. One day he heard a cry, "The earth is on fire! The planet is burning up!" He wanted to help, but he needed to finish his home first. At last it was done. But when he looked around, there was nowhere to put it, for the earth was no more.

Talk together: I once told this story and afterwards asked, "Hearing this story, for what would you pray?" Lucy replied, "A new world." Frank said, "A new house." Cody, thinking hard, and older than the others, frowned and asked, "Why pray for a new home when there's no place to put it?" For what would you pray?

Praying for others, for our sisters and brothers, for the earth, are prayers of "intercession." Let us pray now a prayer of intercession:

Prayer: Dear Lord, bless our sisters and brothers, our earth, ourselves, that we may all live as one in harmony and peace and compassion. Amen.

A Sunny Day
Romans 8:26b

"It's raining!" Brad said, sadly.

Mother looked up from packing the picnic basket and said, "Yesterday the weather woman said, 'A sunny day.' I'm sorry, Brad."

"Maybe it will stop and we can still go to the beach," Brad said, hopefully, as Mother suggested they turn on the weather station and listen: "A new front has entered the area bringing cooler weather and rain. The rain will continue throughout the day."

Mom turned off the radio and began to unpack the picnic basket as Brad ran to his room. On the way he shoved Muffins with his foot and slammed the door. All week Brad had looked forward to going to the beach and building sandcastles in the sand. Now he was stuck at home.

He watched the raindrops run down the window as sliding tears down a sad face. "I know!" he said, suddenly. "I'll pray." Brad kneeled beside his bed and said, "Dear God, Mom and I have planned to go to the beach today. Could you please stop the rain and send it instead tomorrow? Amen."

Brad opened his eyes. The sky was still crying.

The rest of the day Brad grumbled and complained. On Sunday, walking into his church school room, Mrs. Lewis greeted him. "Hi, Brad!" Annie cried, but Brad did not speak. He had to tell Mrs. Lewis. "God doesn't love me," he said to her. Annie came over to listen. Mrs. Lewis asked, "Why do you say that, Brad?"

"I prayed for a sunny day and it rained all day."

Before Mrs. Lewis could respond, Annie said, "Oh, but, Brad, you have to take turns! The farmers wanted rain."

Talk together: Have you ever felt as Brad, that God didn't love you?

Prayer: Help us, Lord, to remember to "take turns." Amen.

Brother Lawrence
Psalm 150:6

The greasy, sticky pots and pans were piled precariously on the sink. The potatoes and carrots, beans and peas were stacked on the floor beside the sink when Brother Lawrence came into the kitchen from morning prayers. He said, "Ah, Brother Sink, you look full this morning and very pleased." As he scrubbed the pots and pans, Brother Lawrence sang:

"Praise God from whom all blessings flow.
Praise God all creatures here below.
Praise God above ye heavenly hosts.
Praise God and Christ and Holy Ghost! Amen."

His singing filled the small, sunny kitchen all the morning. When the pots shone with cleanliness and the pans were scrubbed and put away, Brother Lawrence spoke to the vegetables on the floor. "Now, Brother Potato, it is time for your bath. Sister Carrot, how happy you must be that God has dressed you in such a joyful color. Brother Bean and Brother pea, you may have the same color, but each of you is unique in your shape. Praise God we are not all alike!" Brother Lawrence again began singing as he washed the vegetables, knowing he was in the presence of God.

Talk together: Have you ever talked to a potato or a pea? Do you know the song Brother Lawrence sang? It is called the "Doxology." We can sing it together now.
Sing the doxology.

Prayer: Dear God, fill us with the love and joy of Brother Lawrence. Help us do our work with his joy and song. Amen.

Forgive Us Our Trespasses
Luke 11:4

Once Abraham invited a beggar to his tent for a meal. When the prayer was being said, the beggar shouted, "There is no God! If there is, cursed be God's name!" The beggar was angry at God, for he blamed God for everything that had happened to him, even for his own laziness. Abraham stared at the man and said, "Look around at God's creation and be glad. Thank God for life which is the greatest gift God gives us." The beggar only repeated, "Cursed be God's name!" Abraham stood up and told the beggar to leave his tent, and the beggar left. That night while Abraham was praying, God said to him, "Where is the beggar I sent you?" Abraham replied, "I sent him away. He cursed your name, O Holy One." Then God said, "Abraham, that man has cursed me every day for fifty years and yet I fed him. Could you not put up with him for one single night?"

Talk together: In the Lord's prayer we say, "Forgive us our trespasses as we forgive those who trespass against us." Why do we forgive?

Prayer: Dear Lord, help us forgive and thank you for forgiving us. Amen.

Teach Us To Pray
Matthew 14:22-33

In our Bible story for today, Jesus went up the mountain by himself to pray.

Touring the Cathedral in Washington, D.C., the family could not enter the altar area because a group was there praying for peace. Six-year-old Sarah insisted that her family do so, as well. After all, weren't they for peace? They toured the rest of the Cathedral and when they finished, Sarah was still determined to join the group in prayer. Knowing Sarah's persistence, her mother agreed and together they entered the altar area. The prayers were spoken aloud and were all the same because they centered on one thing: peace. Sarah said her prayer for peace, listened a few minutes and whispered to her mother, "Let's go."

When her mother told me this story, I recalled taking Sarah to church when she was three. As we entered the church, there was a large mosaic of Jesus and the children beside a small pond, which had become Sarah's "wishing well," filled with pennies. Every Sunday, when we arrived, we threw in pennies and wished. One Sunday Sarah threw her pennies into the pond, looked up at the mosaic, and prayed aloud, "Jesus, take care of the children." Sarah's words, like arrows, flew straight into the heart of God.

Talk together: Jesus prayed. His prayers to God were "Thy will be done" and not for his wants, just as Sarah prayed for the children. For what or whom do you pray?

Prayer: Dear Lord, take care of the children and teach us to pray. Amen.

The Lord's Prayer In "New Haven"
Luke 11:2-4

Once upon a time in a town called "New Haven," the mother sat on her son's bed and they talked together about the good things and the bad things that had happened that day. Then Bill's mother explained to him that in prayer Bill could talk with God that same way.

Bill listened and nodded his head. He knew about talking with God. That was the way he prayed.

"Mommie, last Sunday I learned the way Jesus' friends prayed. It's called 'The Lord's Prayer.' "

His mother asked, "Would you like to pray it now?"

Bill nodded his head again and said, "Our Father, which art in New Haven, how do you know my name?"

The mother kissed Bill good night, turned out the light, and left the door open.

The next day she went to her minister. She was worried about Bill's prayer.

The minister asked, "What is it?"

Bill's mother replied, "Our Father, which art in New Haven, how do you know my name?"

The minister said, "I wouldn't change a word of the way he says the Lord's Prayer, for it shows he understands two important things about God: first, that God is very near, in New Haven (in our hometown), second, that God knows him closely, personally knows his name."

Talk together: Does God know your name?

"Our Father who art in heaven ..." Some young children think God's name in heaven is "Art," and some, hearing "hallowed be your name," think God's name is "Harold." What do you call God?

Prayer: Thank you, God, for being near and knowing my name. Amen.

115

The Lord's Prayer
Luke 11:14

One day Jesus sat in the garden with a friend. The air was still. The garden was quiet. Neither of the two men spoke. Suddenly Jesus closed his eyes. His friend became sad because he knew that Jesus was far away from him, and when Jesus closed his eyes to pray, he received a special power. Oh, how he wanted this same power — more than anything in the world! Jesus' friend was very strong, but he knew Jesus had a special strength that gave him great courage. He wanted to know that secret! Yet he had never asked Jesus. The man thought to himself, "He would refuse me. He would laugh at me," and so the man was afraid to ask.

When Jesus opened his eyes, the man looked into them and saw compassion and love and wondered why he had been afraid. He knew Jesus loved him, but did he love him enough to tell him the secret of his power? The man shook his head, sadly. But when he looked at Jesus again, he knew that part of that power was his love. He stuttered as he spoke, "I ... I ... would you ... could you ..."

Then all in one breath, he said, "Would you share the secret of your power?"

Jesus looked up at him and smiled, and said, "When you pray, say, 'Our Father who is in heaven, blessed be your name. Your kingdom come, your will be done, on earth as it is in heaven. Give us today our daily bread. Forgive us our wrongs, as we forgive those who do us wrong. And lead us not into temptation, but deliver us from evil. For yours is the kingdom, the power, and the glory!' This is the secret of my power, my prayer."

Prayer: Let us pray together now, using the words Jesus used, which we call "The Lord's Prayer." Amen.

In The Presence Of God
Psalm 13

"But, Grandma, I gave all of my Halloween candy but the M and M's to Brad," she gulped between tears. "It's not fair, Grandma! He got all my candy, and now he took my M and M's!"

It was Thanksgiving Day and both children were hungry, awaiting the special meal. I had seen Brad grab the package of candy out of Lauren's hands. He was older and bigger and her only defense was tears, because it was not an incident my son, their dad, had time to settle, since he was the chief cook in the kitchen with ten minutes before we sat down to eat.

Lauren and I sat on her bed. Being a "rescuer" and hating "unfairness," I heard myself saying, "It isn't fair, Lauren, but I will get you a large package of many small packages in exchange for the one taken from you." There were more tears before the logic of "more" was understood.

Now, keeping my promise, wrapping the M and M's, I wondered at what I had done. I had tried to solve Lauren's problem with a "material" gift. Yet when the most traumatic experience of disappointment happened to me, it was neither money nor material things that brought me healing. It was prayer, God's promise of love.

I promised myself that the next time Lauren was in tears because of unfairness and helplessness, we will pray together. It may not calm her the first time, nor the tenth. She is only six. On the other hand who knows what might happen ... in the presence of God.

Talk together: Have you ever experienced something that was unfair? What happened? What did you do?

Prayer: Dear Lord, help us remember to trust in your steadfast love when unfairness happens, or we are hurt or disappointed. Amen.

Scripture Index